G000138781

SEEDS FOR THE SOUL

This book is dedicated to my friend, Jed De Torres.
He has always remained faithful to God
constantly nourishing others
with his gift of faith through singing and teaching.
Thank you for witness of faith especially in the difficult times.

Brendan McGuire

Seeds for the Soul

SUNDAY HOMILIES FOR CYCLE A

Maureen,

May these words bring you
ever closer to the Word of
god, Christ himself

God Bless

Fr. Brendan

the columba press

First published in 2007 by
the columba press
55A Spruce Avenue, Stillorgan Industrial Park,
Blackrock, Co Dublin

Cover by Bill Bolger
Cover picture by Jed deTorres
Origination by The Columba Press
Printed in Ireland by ColourBooks Ltd, Dublin

ISBN 978 1 85607 589 3

Acknowledgements:
I am very grateful to the authors, editors and publishers of the following resources which have been inspirational to me and on which I have
drawn in the course of preparing this book. I strongly recommend them
to readers: *Celebration: An Ecumenical Worship Resource*, (Kansas City,
Montana: National Catholic Reporter Company, Inc.); *Connections*
(Mediaworks, Londonderry, NH.); *Homily Helps*, (St Anthony
Messenger Press: Cincinnati, OH.); Brian Cavanaugh, *The Sower's Seeds*,
and *Fresh Packet of Sower's Seeds*, (Mahwah, New Jersey: Paulist Press,
1990); DeMello, Anthony SJ, *One Minute Nonsense*, (Chicago: Loyola
University Press, 1992); Fr Damien Dougherty OFM, *Scripture
Commentaries for Christmas*, (Online through liturgy.com); James S.
Hewett, *Illustrations Unlimited*, (Wheaton, New York: Tyndale House
Publishers, 1988); Jude Siciliano OP, *Preachers Exchange*, (Raleigh, NC:
preachex@opsouth.org); Liam Lawton, *Light the Fire*, (Chicago, IL: GIA
Publications, 1995); Nicky Gumbel, *Questions of Life*, (Cook
Communications Ministries: Colorado Springs, Colorado, 1996); Walter
J. Burghardt SJ, *Tell the Next Generation*, (New Jersey: Paulist
Press,1980); William F. Maestri, *Grace Upon Grace*, (Makati, Philippines:
St Paul Publications, 1988); William J. Bausch, *Story Telling the Word*,
and *More Telling Stories Compelling Stories*, (Mystic, Connecticut:
Twenty-Third Publications, 1996).

Copyright © 2007, Brendan McGuire

Contents

Introduction

I believe that God's ways are mysterious yet understandable, hidden yet knowable, and divine yet human. In the struggle to understand God's ways we need to reflect on his role in our lives. We need to take the time to listen to him speak through the daily events of our lives. The only way we experience life is through our human and fragile efforts, and so, it is in the midst of the ordinariness of life that I believe God speaks to us. He speaks loudly yet clearly if 'we have ears to hear'. Throughout the gospels, Jesus speaks in parables that are enigmatic, yet comprehensible; his meaning is concealed, yet intelligible; the knowledge he shares emanates from God, yet is for us with our human fallibility and frailty. Our task is to listen to God's Word, and then reflect on how his Word relates to our ordinary everyday lives.

The title of this book was inspired by the Parable of the Sower of Seeds, from Matthew 13. The seed of the Word of God is proclaimed every week at Mass throughout the world, but we still do not fully understand the power of God's Word in our lives. This book is the third in a series of three. Nearly all of these homilies were delivered, in person, to communities of faith in San Jose and Santa Clara, California.

My hope is that the stories in this book will help those of you who read them find a place in your soul to plant the seed of God, and that somewhere, at some time, on your journey through life, you will allow God to water this seed and bring it to fruition. May God bless your reflection and the 'planting of the seed'.

Acknowledgements
Each week my homily for the Sunday Mass starts with a story that somehow breaks open the scripture readings. The story is connected to the lives of the parishioners to whom the homily is preached and then connected to God's story. The typical conclusion of a homily will be some form of challenge for our personal lives throughout the week ahead. Then, after it is edited several

times, I send the homily via electronic mail to a list of people who have requested it. One of those friends, Audry Lynch, an author herself, asked me to consider collecting my weekly homilies and getting them published. She then put me in contact with Seán O Boyle of The Columba Press. Thank you to Seán O Boyle and Brian Lynch for their patience with me.

As part of the process of developing the right message, each week I 'bounce' my ideas off some friends. And for the last few years, Jed De Torres has listened patiently, critiqued gently and reacted strongly to my ideas. I wish to express my gratitude to him for his patience, kindness and inspiration; his wisdom is now embedded in these homilies. The cover of this book was also designed and painted by Jed De Torres.

Additionally, I want to thank the staff and parishioners of Holy Spirit Parish in San Jose, California for their support over the past four years. They have given me inspiration by their depth of faith, especially those in the daily Mass community. In a special way I want to acknowledge Karen Boyd and Penny Warne, who spent endless hours editing and proofing the texts of these homilies. Without their help this book would not have been a reality.

Finally, I want to again thank my closest brother Paul and his wife Maria and their three children, Daniella, Dominic and Sean, who are the source of great love and truly the source of inspiration for so many homilies. Their friendship and love sustains me from week to week. Thank you.

Live Fully in the Present

After spending some time over these last few days with my niece and nephew, age seven and five, I realise that children have a completely different concept of time than adults. Let me give you an example. When I arrived for Thanksgiving Day dinner on Thursday I gave my niece and nephew a little gift of chocolate. They immediately wanted to open and eat it. Instead I said they had to wait until after dinner. Fortunately they did not argue and accepted the condition. Of course, as soon as the last mouthful of dinner was eaten the first question out of their mouths was 'Can we eat the chocolate now?' My brother said they had to wait five minutes. Well, you would think we said wait till the end of the world! Every thirty seconds they asked, 'Is it five minutes yet?' 'No you still have four minutes and thirty seconds?' 'Is it five minutes yet?' they persisted. 'No you still have four minutes!' Eventually the five minutes were up and they were allowed to eat the chocolate. They consumed the chocolate as if they had starved for weeks enjoying every bit with great glee. They anticipated that moment so much and savoured every second of eating that chocolate. It was so funny to see.

We could learn something from children of this age and how they live in the present moment. They do not seem to worry about the future nor do they dwell on the past. They simply enjoy the present for what it is and anticipate it with joy. My niece and nephew eagerly awaited that moment and were totally consumed by the moment when it finally arrived. They relished every ounce of the chocolate.

Today's readings focus on the message of time and how precious our time here on earth is. The prophet Isaiah tells us of a time of peace for all nations, when the mountain of the Lord will be visible to all. The time will come when we put our total faith in God. In the letter to the Romans, Paul challenges his disciples to wake up from sleep and not to live in the darkness of their sin. Instead, they are called to live in the light of Christ and spend their precious time wisely and joyfully. In the gospel, we are told to always be prepared for the return of the Lord in glory. We are to live each day as if it was our last. Be always ready for the Lord.

But it seems, at times, to be challenging to us to live in the present. It is hard for us to let go of our past hurts and pains because they seem ever so real. It is hard for us to not worry about the future whether it's our own financial security or that of our children. It is especially hard to live in the present when we have so many gifts to buy and so many things to get ready for the coming Christmas season. Yet, we often only appreciate what we have when it is gone. We appreciate our health only after getting ill. We appreciate the love of friends only after losing it in some way. We appreciate our lives only after we realise how old we are getting. Yes, we find it so hard to fully live in the present moment. But it does not need to remain like that.

This season of Advent is an opportunity to reflect on the time we have. It is a time to know that Christ once came in the form of a human person and he will come again in glory. In the interim, we are called to live life to the fullest with the joyful anticipation of his arrival. In the interim, we are called to live our lives according to the gospel. Each week we come to this table to celebrate that message and take away with us the joy of his presence in the world. We are called to live fully the message of joy in the present moment. Today and this week, we can live joyfully by accepting the gift of our present time without dwelling on the past or worrying about the future. Today may we prepare for Christ's second coming by acting like little children and living fully in the present.

Advent 2A Sunday
Isaiah 11:1-10; Psalm 72; Romans 15:4-9; Matthew 3:1-12

Looking at the Root Cause

There is a story told of a young boy named Bobby, who had just started kindergarten when his parents noticed something disturbing. Every day Bobby would bring home pictures he had drawn at school. But all his pictures were coloured only in black and brown. Not wanting to needlessly upset Bobby, his parents did not ask him directly about the colours; instead they scheduled an appointment with a child therapist to see if there was something emotionally bothering their son.

At their first meeting, the therapist asked Bobby about colouring. Bobby went on and on about how he loved to colour at school and how he would bring his drawing home to Mom and Dad. The therapist suggested to his parents that they give Bobby some more time to adjust to his new school. Nothing changed! The therapist then put Bobby through a battery of psychological tests, but everything was fine. Again, she recommended giving Bobby more time. Still nothing changed.

The therapist decided to take a different tack. She set up a small table in her office with drawing paper and the biggest box of crayons she could find – 96 of the most brilliant colours. When Bobby came in, he headed straight for the crayons and asked if he could draw. 'Sure, Bobby,' said the therapist, 'draw anything you like.' Bobby sat down and tore open the new box. 'Boy, they are great! Better than what I have at school.' The therapist was excited because she thought that she made an emotional breakthrough. She pulled up a little chair and said to Bobby, 'I notice that you are using lots of colours in your drawing today. What do you like about these crayons that you don't like about the crayons at school?' Bobby responded, 'The crayons at school are all brown or black!'[1]

Our society today is better at dealing with symptoms rather than facing the real cause of problems. Even in our own lives, we often deal with symptoms rather than investigating the root cause of our problem. It is not until there is a trend of overbearing pain that we really take stock of what is happening. For example, if we get a headache, we take a Tylenol tablet. Or if we

---

1. 'Connections' (Mediaworks, Londonderry, NH: November 2004)

have a pain in the knee, we take a Motrin tablet. If, however, the headache lasts for weeks or the pain in the knee is so bad that we can no longer walk then we need to look at what is really causing the pain. Only then do we really deal with the issue.

In today's gospel, John the Baptist was so excited because he knew the Messiah was here. He was sure that the world of peace foretold in the book of Isaiah would be realised in and through Jesus Christ. John was telling his disciples they needed to repent for the kingdom of God was at hand. But they also needed to turn back towards God. We need to realise that being a disciple is more than 'not sinning'. We need to face the real problem in our lives and turn back towards God. To simply stop sinning is equivalent to dealing with only the symptoms. But turning back towards God and being totally committed to God is looking for the real cause of our problem. That requires a whole change in our way of life. In general, I think we do quite well as individuals asking God's forgiveness for our times of weakness. However, there is also a community aspect we need to address.

When the Sadducees and Pharisees came seeking John's baptism, he challenged them to deal with the real root of their sinfulness. He zinged them with a scorching accusation, 'You brood of vipers … produce good fruit as evidence of your repentance.' It was not enough that they sought forgiveness. They needed to provide evidence of their real conversion. For John, real discipleship was a total change in life. It was a turning away from the old way of life and turning back towards God. This world that Isaiah foretold was a world very different: 'Where the wolf will lie down with the lamb,' and required a radical change in the system as well. He challenged them to examine the real cause of their sinfulness and for him it was the very structure they belonged to, their synagogues.

I tried to illustrate the community aspect of discipleship in my article in the bulletin last week, I explained the difference between social outreach and social justice. Outreach treats the symptoms and is very action oriented. We often call this charity. These services respond to immediate needs. Some examples are visiting the homebound, feeding the hungry, advent angels, clothing drives, and serving the needs of the grieving. Social justice is aimed at the root cause of an issue – challenging social structures that are unjust. Some examples are right to life advocacy, dignity of life, economic justice, voter registration, housing, labour and many other issues. It seems to me that we are pretty good at charity, but when it comes to social justice, we fall short. We don't often think about the root cause of problems. Today's scripture challenges us to prepare the way for the Lord, both in our own lives as well as in the structures and institutions to which we belong.

This week as we prepare for Christmas by buying lots of gifts for our families and friends (that is a good thing in itself), can we also be aware of the injustice in our world? Can we balance how much spend on ourselves versus giving in charity and/or volunteering to be involved? We need to realise that ninety percent of the world's wealth belongs to the top ten percent of the population. For the most part, we belong to that ten percent and we ought to ask how we can help change the system. There will be children across America who will not eat on Christmas day and will have to go hungry. There will be children across the world who will not eat for another week. We need to ask why, and do we care enough to find an answer? This week, as we prepare the way of the Lord in our own lives, may we seek the root causes of problems as a society, not just the symptoms.

Go and Tell Others What You See and Hear

Many years ago I had the opportunity to go to the Philippines and it was a wonderful visit. However, before leaving home I had a lot of pre-conceived notions about what to expect when I got there. I mean I thought the Philippines were going to be like Singapore with its wealthy shopping areas and beautiful downtowns. Indeed, Manila was a lot like that and much more. They have the 'Shoemart Mall' which must be one of the largest malls in the world. It covers six blocks and is five stories high. It seems to go forever in every direction. But right next to the Mall is an area of extreme poverty where people live in slums. Both coexist side by side.

My pre-conceived notions of the Philippines were shattered by the true reality. One of my friends was a priest working in one of these slums and I had the great fortune to spend some time with him while he worked. What struck me most about this new reality was the generosity of the people. I mean, no matter how little the people seemed to have, they were always willing to share it with others who had less. In these slums there was a caring for one another that one rarely sees. It was not just in the slums but also throughout the country that people genuinely cared about others and tried to help them. It was quite a lesson.

I am sure that you have travelled somewhere with certain expectations, only to find yourself completely shocked by the true reality. Or maybe it was meeting someone famous and your expectations were very different from the reality.

In today's gospel, John the Baptist had some expectations of how the Messiah was going act and who he was going to be. While he proclaimed that Jesus was the Messiah, he had expected him to be a prophet like him. John lived an austere life in the desert preaching with fire and brimstone and condemning those who would not turn back to God. On the other hand, Jesus preached a message of love and forgiveness. Instead of condemning the sinners, he forgave them. He even dined with sinners and one of his disciples was a chief tax collector. Instead of advocating austerity, Jesus criticised those who flaunted their fasting before others. When asked if he was the messiah, he simply responded by saying, 'Look at my actions. The blind see, the deaf hear, the lame walk, lepers are cleansed, and the poor have the good news proclaimed to them.' He wants others to judge his ministry by his actions and not by some preconceived notions of what it should be! Then he promises the kingdom of God to all who follow him.

We are called to follow the Lord by imitating his actions. We are called to be agents of healing and reconciliation. We are reminded in the second reading from the Letter of James, not to judge one another so that we may not be judged. We need to suspend our preconceived notions of others and find a way to minister to them. Whether it is people of another country in their country or whether it is people of another country in our country. Or whether it is a group of people within our community who are of a different race, creed, political party or orientation. No matter who they are, the gospel is preached to all people everywhere.

I wonder if someone were to ask us a similar question that was asked of Jesus: 'Are you a Christian? Or do we need to seek another?' Would we be able to respond to them in the same way Jesus did? 'Look at what I do and judge for your self.' I suspect most of us would not be able to say it so quickly. But we can become agents of healing and reconciliation. We hope that we can say as a community that we visit the sick or imprisoned, we make time for those who are lonely or homebound, we reach out to the homeless and rejected. We may not bring about miracles of sight to the blind or hearing to the deaf, or walking to the lame but we can be agents of healing in the lives of those around us. Whether it is in our offices, schools or homes, whether it is where we work, play or eat, we can be agents of healing in the way we act towards one another.

This week, we can prepare the way of the Lord in our lives by suspending our judgements of others and dispensing with our preconceived notions of who they are meant to be. We can become agents of healing and reconciliation. Today, may we preach the gospel by our actions and say to others, 'Go and tell them what you see and hear.'

Stand By Those in Times of Trouble

Rick Reinhardt was not a particularly nice guy. He was a drug addict. Maybe even a drug dealer. He hung around the wrong people and was regularly in trouble with the law. One day, a few years ago, he was arrested on suspicion of murder. Because of his criminal background it was not difficult to convict Rick of 1st degree murder despite only circumstantial evidence. Everybody who knew him disowned him except for his sister. They wanted nothing to do with him, refusing phone calls and pleas for help. The only person who believed his story was his sister and she convinced a public defender that he was truly innocent. He languished in prison for eighteen months before he got his second chance in court.

Upon further investigation by police, it was concluded that Rick was indeed framed by his best friend. It was a sordid story about murder, betrayal and loyalty. After a speedy second trial, Rick was acquitted of all charges and set free just last week. The only person who gave Rick hope in an otherwise hopeless situation was his sister. She visited him in prison, wrote to him often and even brought her children to visit him. He said that the only hope he had in the dark tunnel of trouble was that comfort to know his sister believed him. Only his sister and his public defender stood by Rick in his time of trouble.

In today's gospel, we hear how Joseph was planning to turn away from his wife-to-be by quietly divorcing her. Mary was pregnant before the marriage. Justice in that time in history would have dictated banishment from her town or city, leaving her to survive on the streets as a prostitute. It would probably have meant shame and banishment for the family too. Indeed, she could have been stoned to death for such an offence. But Joseph chose to protect Mary and her child because he listened when a messenger from God told him that something special was about to happen. It would have been easier to walk away and not get involved after all he was not the cause of this problem. It would have been easier to pretend that the dream was 'just a dream' and to leave Mary alone to take the consequences of her actions. He was righteous in the eyes of the law to divorce Mary or have her cast out of town. Instead he chose to stand by her in her time of need. Instead he chose to listen to that message from God. Instead he chose to offer Mary a home in which to raise this child. Instead Joseph chose to stand with Mary in her time of trouble.

Maybe there are some people in our lives who have made mistakes and need someone to stand by them in their time of trouble. I suspect they will not be accused of murder like Rick Rienhardt and will not be sent to prison for their hideous crimes. But maybe they will be accused of some wrong at work or at home and the consequences for their action will be severe. If it is someone in our family, we may have decided that they are no longer welcome in our lives. If it is someone at work or school, we may have decided they are no longer our friend and refuse to even interact with them. Maybe they really did the dastardly deed and our punishment is a righteous one. While it might be righteous under the Law to punish them, the gospel calls us to be compassionate. The gospel today calls us to stand by them in their time of trouble.

I am not saying that we should stay in dysfunctional relationships. There are times we need to stand our ground for our health and the long term good of the other person. Such examples are that of drug addiction or dysfunctional behaviour where confrontation is the only solution to modify behaviour.

However, most of us will not be dealing with drug addicts this Christmas. Instead, most of us will deal with our families and friends and amongst them we have our own stories of betrayal and unforgiveness. Today the gospel invites us to listen to God as he guides us. God will operate through his own messaging system. He will show us the way if we choose to listen. It may not be through an angel in a dream but it could be through the simple words of a friend or stranger. It could be through the silence of prayer. Whatever it is, we are called to listen to that inner voice guiding us so that we do the will of God in our lives. This week may we hear the gospel challenge and be ready to stand by one of our friends or family members in their time of trouble.

Lift the Fog and Let the Light of Christ Shine

Yesterday in the morning, when we all woke up, there was a very heavy fog over the entire area. The fog was so heavy that we could not see the beauty of the mountains and we were barely able to see the house next door. The fog lasted most of the morning and did not really burn off until today. Look outside today, it is beautiful, the sun is shining brightly and the mountains are dancing in their own majesty, and yes, we can see our neighbours again!

When the fog hung over our neighbourhood, the mountains, hills and neighbours had not disappeared but were merely hidden from view. They were shrouded in a fog of darkness even the sun could not break through.

Then this morning the sun shone brightly and started to burn off the fog. It was slow at first. Soon, most of the fog was gone, although there is still some left in those lower shady valleys. Why does that fog persist? The sun, during the winter months, does not reach very high in the sky, leaving lots of shady areas. The heat of the sun did not touch those valleys and as a result they remained in darkness. To burn off fog, the sun needs to shine its light on that area and the earth itself needs to warm up so the fog dissipates. The fog will always disappear rapidly when both the sun shines and the earth is warmed.

Over 2,000 years ago, humanity was covered by a fog of sin and it shrouded the whole world in darkness. The fog was so heavy that they could hardly see each other, let alone the beauty of the created world around them. Then a Child was born into this created world and he shone his light brightly for all to see. He was the light of the world. God sent his son into the world to burn off the fog of sin and allow us to see the beauty of other humans and the wonder of the created world. As the prophet Isaiah says, 'The people who walked in darkness have seen a great light; upon those who dwelt in the land of gloom a light has shone' (Is 9:1). [The Gospel of John says, 'This life was the light of the human race; the light shines in the darkness, and the darkness has not overcome it… John came for testimony, to testify to the light, so that all might believe through him. He was not the light, but came to testify to the light. The true light, which enlightens everyone, was coming into the world.' (John 1:4)] Christ is that light of the world. He is the Word made flesh for all to see. He is our God made human to show us the way. He is our God made human to know the view behind the fog. He is our God made human so we can see each other again.

Some say that the real meaning of Christmas has been lost, shrouded in an atheistic fog of commercialism. I do not agree at all. The only way that we can lose the meaning of Christmas is if we stop believing in God-made-human in Christ. Then the fog of disbelief can roll in. It does not matter if we say Merry Christmas or Happy Holidays. The only thing that matters is if we truly believe in Christ. God shone his light in this world through the gift of his Son. God so loved the world he gave his Son as a witness to that love. That is how God keeps away the fog of sin, doubt, and hurt. He loves us and shows us how to love one another. If we want to see the real meaning of Christmas, then we are called to love one another.

I am not saying that is easy because it is not easy at all. When the fog of doubt, pain, or sin rolls in, it is hard to keep from shrouding our lives in darkness. Sometimes that fog of doubt appears because we have lost a loved one to death or they have left our lives for other complicated reasons. Sometimes that fog of pain rolls into our lives because of some negative personal interaction that has occurred. Sometimes that fog of sin lingers in the valleys of our lives because of poor judgements or bad choices. Whatever the cause, it is sometimes very hard to keep the fog from hiding the goodness of God and his abundant gifts he gives to us. Sometimes the fog just keeps coming into our hearts and darkness lingers where there should be light.

That is why we need each other and we come together each week at Eucharist. Yes, we come because Jesus commanded us to do so but more than that. We need to come for ourselves. There are those times we cannot keep the fog away on our own. Those are the moments when we need the heat of the gathered community.

Christ was born some 2,000 years ago to show us the light of this world: to burn brightly and cast away the darkness. But also know that we need to cooperate with this light and allow ourselves to be warmed by the action of loving. We know that God's light shines down on us through Christ but we also know that we are now the light of this world. We dispel the darkness of our lives by choosing to love others, even when they hurt us, even when they are gone from our lives, even when they are homeless or destitute. By our loving, forgiving, and believing in each other we can keep away the fog of doubt, pain, and sin and keep the light of Christ burning brightly.

Everlasting Arms of God

There was a pastor who went to visit the home of a young woman whose husband had been buried the day before. They had only been married for three months when he became sick with pneumonia. After severe complications, he died very suddenly, leaving her a widow at a very young age. When the pastor walked into the house the tension rose immediately. There was a white-haired woman sitting in a low chair, her face half-hidden by her hand. Her other hand was caressing the shoulder of the young widow who was sitting on the floor at the foot of a chair. Suddenly, the widow snapped at the pastor ferociously. 'Where is your God?' she demanded. 'I've prayed to him and he is silent now. You preached about his presence in our lives especially in times of trouble. You preached about "His Everlasting Arms". Where are they now?'

With tears in his eyes, the pastor responded by touching the hands of the older woman's arms. 'They are here,' he said in a reassuring tone. 'They are around you even now. These are the arms of your God.'[1]

During Christmas, we celebrate the presence of Christ in our world. And we recognise how important it is to realise that this is more than a single-day event. Christmas is a year-round celebration of Christ alive in the world ... Christ alive in you and me. His everlasting arms are all around us. We heard how Joseph took Mary to be his wife despite her being pregnant by someone other than him. He took her into his house and promised to take care of Mary and her newborn child, Jesus. He stretched out his arms to a woman in need. In today's gospel, we hear how he protects Mary and Jesus again. He wraps his caring arms around her and moves her and Jesus from Bethlehem to Egypt, then to Nazareth, for safety from a vengeful king Herod. Yes, Joseph showed Mary God's everlasting arms.

Christmas is sometimes a difficult time for people who have lost a spouse or a parent, or even harder if they have lost a child. It is also a hard time for families with divisions, as it seems to

---

1. Adapted from 'Connections' (Mediaworks, Londonderry, NH: December, 2004)

emphasise the brokenness of the family unit. This is our opportunity, as members of the Body of Christ, to be the everlasting arms of God to others. It is our opportunity to reach out to others who are hurting or in need of healing. The letter to the Colossians reminds us that, as Christians, we ought to be full of kindness, compassion, gentleness, and forgiveness. We are encouraged to be the hands of healing and the arms of strength to those in need. Maybe we can make a phone call to someone lonely or estranged. Maybe we can write a note to someone who remains distant.

This week, as we remember the powerful witness of the Holy Family to being caring and compassionate to each other, may we remember the example given to us by Joseph and extend our arms to others in need so that God's everlasting arms can become real for someone in need. Today, may we become the everlasting arms of God.

Right Words, Right Time, Right Reason

As many of you know I have a dog, Bubba, who I take for a walk every day in the neighbourhood. He is a friendly dog who likes both other dogs and people. Even so, there are some dogs that don't like him and bark wildly at him. He generally ignores them with a shrug of his shoulder. Yet, if the other dog attacks for any reason, Bubba will protect me at all costs, standing in between the other dog and me. He will do the exactly the same when it comes to humans whom he detects are being hostile to me. He really is very protective of me. That is great, but I need to be careful. On a few occasions, he has taken bites from dogs that were really attacking me. Nothing serious, but I need to be careful.

Recently, we were walking in the neighbourhood and from the side yard of one the neighbours appeared this Doberman Pincher. He launched himself full speed at us with fury and anger. Bubba took his defensive position, placing himself between the oncoming dog and me, growling to fend off the attacker. I saw a disaster about to happen and did what I thought was best. I faced the dog head-on and sternly shouted, 'No!' The dog stopped in mid-tracks. I then added, 'sit,' and he sat. Then I added, 'stay' and he stayed. I couldn't believe what I was seeing. Here was this vicious dog sitting in the middle of the street waiting politely for the next command. I walked away slowly, checking over my shoulder to see if the dog would move at all. Nope! We were all the way to the end of the street and he was still sitting in the middle of the road. Now I was worried that he might get run over by a car! It is amazing what the right words, at the right time, with the right intention, can produce. Yes, familiar words are powerful when used well.

Today's scripture is all about the right words, at the right time, for the right reason. In the first reading from the Book of Numbers, we hear how God gives his blessing through the words of the priests of Israel, the sons of Aaron. These words of blessing date back to 800 BCE and are often used in many modern blessings. The words were particularly powerful since the Israelites were in need of favour from God. Remember, that for the Jews to speak any words was to give life to those words. To ask 'God to bless and keep you, let his face shine upon you' would have been especially important words to be given life. Yes, these were the right words, at the right time, with the right intention.

In today's second reading from Paul's letter to the Galatians, we hear how a single word can change a relationship forever. That word is 'Abba', 'Father'. It redefines our entire relationship with God. Since Jesus Christ was his Son and he told us to pray like him, 'Abba' makes us adopted sons and daughters through Christ. We are no longer slaves but we are children of God and we have the Holy Spirit dwelling within us. Yes, these were the right words, at the right time, with the right intention.

In the gospel of Luke, we hear the shepherds witness to the words spoken to them by an angel. These words were fulfilled in their hearing and they came to believe in Jesus the Christ, the Messiah lying in a manger surrounded by poverty, not in a palace. Mary, upon hearing all this, kept these words in her heart and reflected upon them for her lifetime. Yes, these were the right words, at the right time, with the right intention.

These words echo for us the simple words of Mary, as we recall the Solemnity of Mary the Mother of God, when the angel came to her to announce her new child: 'Let it be done to me according to your word.' Yes, surely these were the right words, at the right time, with the right intention. This response by Mary changed humanity forever. 'Yes words' have incredible power when used well.

We believe, as Christians, that the word of God is the powerful word we hear each week. And yet, those words only become fulfilled in our hearing if we listen to them and heed their call to action. We know that the use of certain words have the power to lift up or to tear down. Think of a person who is suffering from illness or depression, a few kind words chosen at the right time can lift them up out of the fog of pain or depression, if only for a few minutes. Then think of a child who is in need of affirmation, a few unkind words said at the wrong time could take a lifetime to undo. Yes, we have the power to lift up or tear down with our words. It is our choice how we use them.

January 1st is always 'World Day of Peace' and we are called to be promoters of peace in every way. Our words need to be words of peace. I am not suggesting that any of us are inciting world war, but I think in the circles of our own families and friends we can occasionally choose words of war and hostility or at the very least unkind words chosen for the wrong reasons. Instead, we are called to use words that heal, words that will forgive, and words that promote love.

Today and this week, may we know the power of every word we utter. May we choose our words carefully, knowing that we have the power to lift up or to tear down. May our words be the right words of forgiveness, used at the right time of healing, with the right intention of love. It is our choice to use the right words, at the right time, with the right intention.

Shine the Light of Christ Fully

Imagine that I took you into a dark room with no windows, closed the door behind us and told you that I had a light. What would be your response? Of course! Turn on that light. Then imagine if I only turned on the light a little, barely enough for you to see your hand in front of you. What would your response be then? Yes! Turn up the light more. It would be silly to have a light in a dark room and not use it at all, or use it only a little. The purpose of the light is to see.

The same is true of our journey as Christians. We believe that Christ is the light of the world and we have that light shining within us through his Holy Spirit. Yet, we settle ourselves with a little or no light. We rarely let that light of Christ shine before others. We settle ourselves with the dimmer switch on low. We rarely talk about God explicitly with our children, parents, friends, or co-workers. We rarely talk about God in the work place. We, as Catholics, rarely pray in public. When was the last time that we were in a restaurant and we stopped to pray aloud before our meal? I often see other Christian families doing so, why can't we, Catholics, do so too? Yes, we need to let the light of Christ shine brightly in our lives. And the best way to share our faith and belief in Christ is in our every day actions with each other.

John the Baptist was not the light but he came to testify to it. He knew that Christ was the light of the world and wanted others to know that reality. Then Christ came along and said to his disciples that they will be the light of the world after he goes. That means that you and I, as his disciples, are the light of the world today. It is our role to shine the light of Christ before others. We ought to shine it brightly and not on dimmer mode. We do this best by our actions.

The second reading today from the letter to the Ephesians, gives us a great lesson in how we are to act as the light. It tells us to always be prayerful and never cease in giving thanks. We are called to remain thankful no matter what else is going on in our lives. That is not always easy because life often throws us some curve balls. We may be at odds with a relative or friend but we are called to move beyond it. We are challenged to always be grateful for every gift, like our children even when they are rascals, like our parents even when they are needy, like our friends even when they let us down. We ought to be grateful for the many gifts of every day.

We are reminded to pray without ceasing. You have heard me say it a million times, we need to find time to pray outside of this Sunday Mass. Yes, it is wonderful that we are here at church and I thank God that you come each week. But it is not enough! We also need to pray somewhere during the week as well. Pray as individuals and as families. We come to this table each week to receive this nourishment but it is in our everyday lives that we are called to live the liturgy.

This week as we leave here, may we know that we are called to be the light of Christ. We are called to testify to that light by our words and actions, by what we say and what we do. May we not be afraid of praying in public, or sharing our faith with someone in need. But in all things may our actions shine the light first. This week may we let our light shine brightly before all. No dimmed lights this week. Shine brightly for all to see.

Take the Risk and See the Light of Christ

Last year, a friend and I went to Yellowstone National Park. It is a beautiful place with many interesting sites. One such beautiful site is Shoshone Lake. Unfortunately, it was our last day and we had not seen the lake yet. It had rained heavily all morning until late afternoon so our chances were not looking good. Around 5 pm the sun broke through the clouds a little and I said to my friend that we should take the risk and hike the 5 miles. He reminded me of the danger of another thunderstorm or, more importantly, of the real danger of the bears who like to feed in the evening. We are, after all, good food!

We decided to take the risk anyway and we hiked with a pep-in-our-step through the evening twilight. When we arrived, the evening sun glistened off the water and the lake shone like a pot of gold at the end of a rainbow. It was truly magnificent! I will always remember that stunning sight. On the way back, which we made in even quicker time, we congratulated each other on taking the risk over impending dangers, recognising that we were truly rewarded for our efforts.

I think there are many times in our lives when we are presented with opportunities to do good and to be part of something better. But we must be willing to take the risk and be willing to go for it. We must be willing to listen to the message and experience something new.

In today's gospel, we hear about the Magi who saw the birth of a star. They believed that this heavenly wonder symbolised the birth of a heavenly person. They took the risk and followed that star as their sign. After arriving at their destination, they were rewarded with seeing the newborn King of Jews, Jesus Christ. They discovered the new light of the world. And they were forever different! This conversion, symbolised in the story by the change in their return path, caused them to avoid King Herod, whom represented their past. Now they were different. They had seen the light of Christ.

Today, we celebrate the Solemnity of the Epiphany of the Lord, which signifies the manifestation of the light of Jesus Christ, the revelation of Jesus Christ as the Saviour of the world. Isaiah reminds us of that symbolism when he says, 'Arise, shine, for the glory of the Lord has risen upon you' (Is 60:1). This is a celebration of the bright light of Jesus Christ and a reminder that his light still shines today.

We are reminded of our baptism call to see his light shine in all. We are called to see signs of his presence among us. We are called to take the risk and follow his signs. We are called to discover the Christ again. Each of us is different and we see different signs. Where is God guiding us this week? What risk do we need to take to see Christ's light?

Let me give you an example. Just before Christmas our youth group fed the homeless and hungry at our neighbouring parish. At first they were nervous and a little afraid; after returning they were different. Their faces shone brightly as they recalled their experience. They had seen the light of Christ in those they served. Their lives were forever different. We, too, become different when we see the light of Christ present among us. We, too, are never the same. But we have to take the risk!

Maybe it is not feeding the homeless or hungry. Maybe it is, or maybe it is some other ministry in the church that calls us. Perhaps it is someone closer to home. Christmas holidays are always a time of family. When there is division in the family, then this time of year can be difficult. How about we make the light of Christ shine in our families by forgiving someone or reconciling with someone?

Whatever the sign that Christ gives us, may we take the risk and follow it. This week may our hearts be converted again to the Lord and may we discover the light of Christ.

River of Life

There is a powerful Native American story about the importance and holiness of water. The clouds, according to the tale, are Father Sky's gift to Mother Earth. When the clouds are full, they open, and a raindrop falls to Mother Earth. It joins other drops and they become a trickle. The trickle becomes stream and the stream becomes a river. Then the river flows into the ocean. The sun smiles upon the ocean and some of its water turns to mist. It rises toward Father Sky, where the mist becomes a cloud. And when the cloud is full, it opens again and another raindrop falls to Mother Earth. It is not the same raindrop, but it comes from the same ocean. Then it begins its journey to the ocean and one day, back to Father Sky.

The ancient natives believed that you and I are like raindrops. We are all made of the same holy stuff, the water that is life itself. In our own time, our mothers give birth to us and we 'drop' to earth. Each of us is unique. Each of us possesses our own identity. But we are all part of what has gone before us and what comes after us. In some way, we are all connected to each other. And in time, we join others in the streams of our lives. We journey back to the same ocean and back to Father Sky. The water we travel, the water we are, is the Body of Christ. In the waters of the Sacrament of Baptism, we begin that journey back to God who gives us life in the first place.[1]

In waters of baptism, we embrace the name of 'Christ' and the Spirit of his gospel. That gospel unites all of us to the saints who have gone before us and all the saints who will come after us. In these baptismal waters, we join that Body of Christ as we travel through life's deserts and meadows, in struggling trickles and powerful rivers, to the ocean where, one day, we shall all 'return' to our God. Along the way, we gather momentum with other raindrops, and form that trickle that becomes a river. One of those formation moments is when we come to this Eucharist where we become more than just a trickle of people. We become the river of life called the Eucharist. It is here that we gain strength by our presence and the presence of Christ among us.

1. Inspired by 'Connections' (Mediaworks, Londonderry, NH: January, 2005)

Today, we celebrate the Baptism of the Lord. Often people do not understand why the Lord needed the baptism of repentance from John the Baptist. Jesus took on the sins of humanity and it was for that reason he was in need of this baptism. Not because of his sinfulness, but because of ours. He showed us the new way with baptism in the spirit, what we call today Christian Baptism. In and through Christ, God became human. But he remained fully divine. That is what we celebrate here today: Christ fully human and fully divine. On Christmas Day, we started the Christmas season and celebrated God becoming human in Christ. Today, we close the Christmas season and celebrate Christ as truly divine while being fully human. Today, we celebrate the beginning of his new mission. And we acknowledge that we have become his adopted children in our own baptism. We recognise that we are raindrops from heaven on our journey back to our Father God.

Also today, we welcome, in a special way, some new raindrops, as the children who are preparing for their First Eucharist are formally welcomed into their preparation for this sacrament. The challenge for us who are already part of the river of life is to not only welcome them, but to be partners with them in their journey of life. We want to help them understand what we already know: that coming to this table each Sunday is a gift and that we truly become what we receive. We become the Body of Christ. We become that River of Life. That is what we want to share with them. And we do so by encouraging them on their journey. Not just today, but every day. So if one of them is sitting next to you, remember them and encourage them on their journey of life. Help them back to the River of Life.

Mirror, Mirror On the Wall[1]

In the movie *Snow White and the Seven Dwarfs*, there is a line that goes: 'Mirror, mirror on the wall, who's the fairest of them all?' The expectation is that a mirror will speak the truth and never lie. Even though, for some of us, we might want it to!

Sometimes we look into the mirror and we do not like what we see. Other times we look into the mirror and deny what we see because we do not want to believe the truth. The mirror cannot but reflect the truth it sees. We would prefer to see something else. We might say: 'O, I wish that part was not true' or 'I wish I looked like this or that' whether it be wrinkles, graying hair or excess weight. The truth is sometimes hard to bear. Yes, the mirror tells us the truth and reflects back what it sees. In a sense the mirror is ideal self-reflection.

Today we begin our annual journey of Lent. It is a time in which we follow the example of Jesus and spend 40 days reflecting on God's role in our lives. It is important to note that during ancient times, the desert was considered to be a place of self-reflection, whether as an individual or as a group or nation. Israel spent 40 years in the desert, reflecting on their collective life and repenting for their many sins. The desert was a place where all the distractions of life are pulled away and we are able to focus on ourselves in some real way.

In this time of Lent, we are called to go into this 'desert of self-reflection'. We are called to find a desert in our lives so that we can reflect on what we have done in the past, who we are now in the present and what we are called to be in the future. We are called to reflect upon our lives as humans and as Christians, and to find our mission in life. To do this task of self-reflection, the church suggests a common approach: the gospel suggests we pray, we fast, and we give alms. But these actions must be authentic and not just done for outward appearances. The prayer ought to be focused on our journey as Christians. Our fasting ought to be authentic. We should fast from the dis-

---

1. Inspired by Patricia Datchuck Sanchez, 'Celebration: An Ecumenical Worship Resource,' (Kansas City, Missouri: National Catholic Reporter Company Inc, March, 2006) p 1.

tractions of our lives so that we see the true reflection of who we really are and come to understand our real mission in life. Our almsgiving ought to be a true sharing of our gifts with others.

Our Lenten journey, then, is to look in the mirror and see who we really are today. When I suggest looking into the mirror, I am not referring to the ordinary mirror because that is just the outside and that part is easy. I mean the mirror of those whom we love. I mean looking into the faces and hearts of our spouses, children, parents and closest friends. If we look into the faces of those around us, we will see a true reflection of whom we have become. We may not like what we see but it is an authentic reflection. Their faces and hearts will not lie if we really want to see.

If I hurt my spouse or child or parent in some way, then that pain will show in their faces and hearts. But we must be ready to really see it. We might want to ignore and deny the reality of that hurt, walking away and demanding them to stop crying; but the pain or hurt does not go away and their faces reflect the reality of who we are to them. Yes, they are a mirror to us in that moment of pain: our spouses, our children, our parents, our closest friends. In others, we will truly see ourselves. Remember that old adage, 'Show me your friends and I will tell you who you are.' Our friends really do give us a reflection of who we are. Fortunately, pain is not all we see when we look into their reflection. It is equally important to recognise the goodness that we are to them and the love we share. For that love and affection is equally as important as the reflection.

This week, as we start our Lenten desert together, may we take seriously the need to look into the mirror of our lives, the mirror of those closest to us and acknowledge and accept what we see. Acknowledge and accept the hurts we have caused them and ask forgiveness for those times of weakness. But also accept the joy and gift of love we have brought to them in being who we are to them. Today, may we look into the mirror of life and truly see!

The 'Master Key' to Life

Years ago, growing up in Ireland, we had some room keys that were huge – at least eight inches long and weighing at least a pound! There was no way you could lose those keys. Since then, keys have gotten much smaller and we even have 'non-key' keys. An example is that of hotel guest keys – they are a piece of plastic similar to a credit card that slides through the lock, giving you a green light to enter. Another example is remote control keys for car doors. You do not even need to touch the car to get in. And if you lose your remote control or spare keys, they have this system called 'On Star' which allows you to call the main office and from satellite they remotely open your car door. Wow! We have come a long way indeed with keys.

When I arrived at this parish, I was given two keys. One key opened all the doors to the parish buildings and the other key opened all the school doors and the gym. Pretty cool! Just two keys open all the doors! What are those keys called? Yes, they are called 'master keys' and they are designed to open a slew of doors, each having their own separate locks. Usually, these 'master keys' are only given to a select few!

Well, God has given all of us the 'master key' of life and with it we can open up any door we want. This key is not given to only a select few but to all. It is called freedom or free will. While the master key opens up many doors, not all doors are created equal. Indeed, behind many doors are things that are not necessarily good for us. The temptation is to open up whatever door feels good. And each of us will be tempted to open different doors!

In today's gospel, Jesus was tempted to open up the doors of power and glory. First, the devil challenges Jesus to show him his power. 'Just change this stone into bread' the devil teases. Flex his power and authority by showing off! The devil then offers him all the tangible power of this world in exchange for Jesus to worship Satan for just a moment! Just turn away for a moment and all the power could be his. Lastly, the devil challenges Jesus again to throw himself off the building and allow God's angels to save him. 'Don't you trust in your God?' the devil challenges Jesus. Again, show off his power for a quick demonstration!

Today, I have received the keys to the parish as a symbol of the power and authority of my office as Pastor. The temptation will always be there to open some doors that ought to remain closed. The temptation will be there to show off my power and authority. My promise today to you, the community of Holy Spirit, is to come to you and talk about the doors we will open together. Together we will decide in prayer, what doors ought to be opened. Some doors that have been closed a long time may need to be opened and some doors that have been open a long time may need to be closed. Together, in prayer, we can decide how we use our master key.[1]

We are all tempted to open up the doors of power and glory. They are not the same doors that tempted Christ, such as changing a stone into bread. Instead, we might be tempted to open different doors of power. We all have power over someone in our lives. Those of us who work in the corporate world know that we have power over those who work for us or with us. We can make their working lives heaven or hell depending upon how we treat them in the office environment. The temptation is to abuse that power for our own good, to demonstrate to others that we have power over them. Christ experienced this same temptation.

Those of us who are parents have power over our children. We can make their lives miserable or happy, if we want. We can abuse the privilege of our authority by opening the door of selfishness, feeding our own personal needs. Children, we have power over our parents, some more than others! We can make our parents' lives miserable or happy especially our elderly parents. We have a lot of power and authority, and which door we open will determine how they experience us. We have power over our friends in the way we treat them. We can open the door of selfishness, servicing our personal needs while giving little attention to their needs. We have power and authority with everyone with whom we have a relationship. We are all tempted to open doors that ought to remain closed.

During these days of Lent, we are invited to open three new doors: the doors of prayer, fasting, and almsgiving. They are interconnected doors that lead to one another. We are encouraged to open up the door of prayer so we can listen to how the Lord is

1. This Mass was presided by the Bishop and was the installation of the author as Pastor.

guiding us in our lives. Then through sacrifice or fasting we can understand the plight of others and be inspired to give to others in need. Yes, we are called to open these new doors of prayer, fasting and almsgiving and keep the doors of temptation closed. We have the master key that opens every door, but it is up to us to choose the door. If we feel we have lost the master key, then we call on God to remotely open up the door through prayer. Today, which door will we open with our master key?

In the Quiet God Whispers to Us

Some months ago, the renowned liturgical music composer from Ireland, Fr Liam Lawton, gave a concert here at the parish. In the session, he explained a song he wrote in honour of the September 11th victims called 'In the Quiet.' He said that life has become increasingly busier each day, yet there is a greater need to search for the deeper meaning in our lives. There is so much noise and bustle that hinders our yearning to listen to the gentle voice of God. There are times, he said, when we yearn to hide away in places and spaces of quiet, to hear that quiet whispering. We have to recognise our need for that quiet space.

In today's gospel, we hear Jesus invite Peter, James, and John to the quiet space on the top of a mountain, a place to spend some time with God in prayer. Jesus often spent time away from everyone, alone in prayer with his heavenly Father. He teaches his disciples the way to prayer, while also revealing his true identity as the Son of God. On the mountain top, the disciples have such a powerful experience that Peter wants it to last forever – he wants to build a tent for Jesus, Moses, and Elijah, symbolising Christ the Messiah, the fulfilment of both the Law (Moses) and the Prophets (Elijah). Peter did not want the experience to stop. Yet Jesus showed them that they must go back down and be busy with the work of the Lord, serving others. Yet the experience forever marks their life. They realise that they must seek God in the quiet.

We, too, ought to realise that we must seek God in the quiet. We are called to pray especially in this Lenten season. I believe that we need to search for a place or space of silence in which to pray. Maybe it is at the beginning of the day before we head off to work or our day's activities. Maybe it is at the end of the day before we go to bed. Maybe it is on the drive to work in which we can turn off the radio and grasp the silence. Maybe it is waiting for an appointment. Whenever it is, this Lent we can seek God in the silence and hear his quiet whisperings. Maybe we can seek God in the quiet. Now, we can listen to that song.[1]

---

1. Liam Lawton, 'In the Quiet' (Chicago, Il: GIA Publications Inc, 2002) CD-524, track 1.

I and Thou

In 1923, the Jewish theologian, Martin Buber, wrote his famous book called *I and Thou*. The main point of Buber's book is that there are two ways of relating to other people in our lives: We can see them as objects – what Buber calls the 'I-it' relationship; or we can see others as having feelings, dreams, and needs like our own – what Buber calls the 'I-thou' relationship.

In his memoirs, Buber tells the story of how he came to this theory. When he was a professor of philosophy at a university in Germany, a young student came to see him with a problem. The student had received his draft notice to serve in the German army in World War I. He was a pacifist by nature and did not want to kill in battle, but he was also a fiercely loyal and patriotic German. He asked Buber what he should do: serve his country and kill against his conscience or claim conscientious objector status and perhaps allow another young man to be killed in his place.

Buber was in the midst of writing a difficult theological-philosophical treatise, and was rather upset at the interruption of his time. The professor snapped at the young man with something like, 'Yeah, that's a serious dilemma; do what you think is right.' And he went right back to his work.

The young man, in despair for lack of guidance, committed suicide. Buber, for the rest of his life, felt a measure of guilt for not being more present to the young man in need, for seeing him only as an interruption and not as a human soul in torment. Buber felt he had sinned against the image of God in that young student by treating him as an object without needs or feelings.[1]

It is so easy to treat others as objects, to measure their worth not by who they are but by what they are able to do for us. We sometimes treat others as objects and not like human beings. We can often see this in the way we treat clerks at stores or waiter/ waitresses or busboys at restaurants or those who clean our homes or tend our gardens or those who disagree with us politically or morally. We can also see it in the way we treat our spouses, parents, children, coworkers, neighbours, or community

---

1. 'Connections' (Mediaworks, Londonderry, NH: February, 2005)

members. We often treat them as objects of usefulness demanding all sorts of unreasonable things and not recognising that they are humans with feelings, too.

The Samaritan woman in today's gospel is one such victim. Her gender, religious background, and nationality made her a non-person in the eyes of Judaism. Her lifestyle made her despicable in her own town. But instead of treating her as an object, Jesus treated her as a human being and offered her the living water of life, calling forth from her a sense of faith and joy. In this faith and joy, she was able to face her own life and she immediately shared the joy and faith with others. Seeing this extraordinary gift of faith, others from the town came to believe in Jesus for themselves.

This weekend we will witness the first of the Lenten scrutinies for the elect and candidates who are joining our Catholic faith. We witness them as our brothers and sisters in faith on their journey. We sometimes consider the RCIA (*Rite of Christian Initiation*) as a programme for others, as if to treat these seekers of faith as objects in a procedure. Instead, we are called to recognise the importance of these days for them and encourage them in faith and joy. We do this by sharing our own faith and joy in all we do for them. We do this by being human bearers of Christ's mystery. But our role does not stop there. We are called to share our faith and joy with everyone we meet each day, whether the store clerk, janitor, gardener, or family member. Remember, we will be judged on how we treat the least of our brothers and sisters.

So, as we come to this table today and receive this living water of faith, may we also take this living water to everyone we meet. May we not treat others like objects that serve our purpose, whether it be the store clerk, waiter, or family member, but instead treat them as humans with feelings. Today, we share our faith and joy by bringing the living water to everyone we meet.

Bright Lights of Christ

I recently had the opportunity to drive on a very straight free-way, where one could see ahead and behind for miles. As I travelled along, I could see this car in the distance driving very slowly in the fast lane with a line of cars behind it. Every driver handled the situation slightly differently and some would do it faster than others. Basically, each car would drive up behind, quite close, and then eventually pass on the inside. When I got to her and passed her, she was driving about 40mph. The extraordinary thing was that she was completely oblivious to the whole thing, not recognising the commotion she had caused. She was blind to the line of cars behind her backed up in traffic. She was blind to all the cars in front of her as they cut her off. She was even blind to all the drivers as they waved to her as they drove by! She was blind to everything. She just hummed along in that fast lane, content in her world and nothing seemed to disturb her world. The only thing that caught her attention was a police car that came right up behind her and turned on the lights to pull her over. I am sure that she got a citation or, at the very least, a warning.

I think our lives can be very much like that. We are content to hum along in the fast lane of our life, completely blind to the whole world around us. We are blind to the struggles that our wife is having with the kids at home. Or we are blind to the issues that our husband is having with people at work. Or we are blind to the peer pressure that our children are having at school. Yes, we are content to hum along in the fast lane of life until someone pulls us over and chews us out. Maybe it is our spouse, child, or parent. Then we realise that we were blind to the real issues at hand.

If I asked you what the gospel story was about today, most of you would say that it was about a man born blind. Actually, he was just a character in the story and the gospel today was about blindness. The blindness pertained not to the man born blind, but to the religious leaders of the day. Okay, they had physical sight but they refused to see the obvious around them. The people were backed up in 'traffic' behind them and people cut them off in front. But they still refused to see. Indeed, even Jesus, the light of the world, came right up behind them and shone his bright light upon them. But they remained blind. They remained blind to the plight of the people in their day. Nothing would disturb them as they hummed along on their narrow path.

Rarely are many of us totally blind. But I think that most of us are a little blind to some of the struggles of those who surround us. Most of us are content to hum along in the fast lane of life, not recognising the struggles of others, not wanting to be disturbed by the commotion going on around us. Maybe we are blind to the struggle of our child, spouse, or parent. Maybe it is the pain of so many of our neighbours who are currently unemployed or underemployed. Maybe it is the pain of someone we know who has recently gone through a divorce or a broken relationship. Or maybe it is the burden of so many of the world's population, oppressed by economic or violent circumstances. Yes, we are content to hum along in the fast lane of life, content in the isolation of our comforts, remaining blind to the struggles of the world.

Well, this season of Lent is a time when the Lord comes up behind us and puts on his bright lights to pull us over. He tells us to watch the traffic of our lives and pay attention to those around us. He gives us a warning to stop our mindless driving! We are not to remain blind to the whole world. Lent is a time for us to reflect more deeply upon our actions and how they impact others. So, today and this week, may we take the time to allow the Lord to pull us over and shine his bright light into the darkness of our lives, to allow the Lord to guide us out of our darkness and into his wonderful light, to allow the Lord to snap us out of our mindless driving. Today, may we pay attention to those around us and not remain blind.

Untie Them and Let Them Go

There once was an old couple who decided to have a garage sale to get rid of all the excess stuff they had in their home. Among the items they put up for sale was an old mirror they had received many years before as a wedding gift. Because of its rather ugly blue-coloured plastic frame, they never found a place in their house where it looked good. Even though it had been in the garage for years, they really did not want to sell it because it was a wedding gift from a close friend. However, its disposal was long overdue and so they put it among the items to be sold. During the sale, a young man saw the old mirror and called his wife over to examine it. They fell in love with it and quickly purchased it at a bargain price.

The old couple helped load the mirror into to the new owners' truck at which time they overheard the new owners chatting. 'Look at this beautiful mirror!'said the husband, 'It even still has its protective cover on the frame!'As he peeled off the ugly blue plastic protective covering, it revealed a beautiful gold-leaf frame. The old couple was in shock as they realised they had a treasure, wrapped up in plastic, for years in their garage.[1]

When we are born into this world, we are all treasures to behold. We are all a gift from God. But often we do not take the opportunity to unwrap our 'plastic covering'and discover the true gifts that we really are. We often add to the wrapping of our lives and bind ourselves with some destructive behaviour, possession, or obsession. We can let our anger, disappointment, pain, sadness, cynicism, and despair bind us up and bury us in tombs of isolation. We decide early in our lives that we lack value, and then live in that reality, often entombing ourselves into the 'garage of life'. We also assess the value of others early on, and often relegate their status to 'less than valuable'. We categorise them as people who 'talk too much', 'are too full of themselves', 'are too talented for their own good', 'are not smart or not good-looking enough', or simply 'we don't like'. Often,

---

1. Adapted from story in 'Connections' (Mediaworks, Londonderry, NH: March, 2005)

we bind them with anger, unforgiveness, or jealousy and we refuse to let them out of the tombs that we have made for them.

Our Lenten journey challenges us to act otherwise. It is a time for conversion of our hearts and minds. It is a time for us to examine the way we view ourselves and others. It is a time to unwrap the 'plastic' of our lives and others' lives to reveal the full potential of us and them. It is a time to unbind ourselves, and others, setting us free from our judgements, prejudices or biases.

In today's gospel we hear about the death and rising of Lazarus. Jesus says 'Lazarus, come out! Untie him and let him go.' He reveals himself as the 'resurrection and the life'. He promises that whoever believes in him will have eternal life. To each of us who believe, he says 'Come out, let yourselves go! Come out and let others go too! Untie yourselves from your bands of lack of self-worth and let yourselves go! Untie others from the bands of your anger, unforgiveness, and jealousy. Unwrap people from the plastic covering into which you have trapped them and let them go free from the entombment of your judgements. Today, let yourselves, and others, go free.'

Passion Sunday
Isaiah 50:4-7; Psalm 22; Philippians 2:6-11; Matthew 26:14-66

God is Always There

Father, if it is possible, let this cup pass from me;
yet, not as I will, but as you will.

Yes, we know that Jesus Christ is truly divine. But rarely do we see the humanity of Jesus more evident than in today's powerful passion narrative. These words of Jesus show the anguish that he feels as he faces his moment of pain and death. We can hear the human emotions of agony in the garden. This moment in the garden shows the depth of the human suffering he was to endure. Yet the human Jesus accepted this pain and suffering so that the whole world would know that God loves them. Jesus accepts the will of the Father not to glamorise pain or suffering but to personally inform us that there is life beyond pain and death.

Lest we romanticise this moment ourselves as something divine and pious, let us put ourselves in Jesus' shoes as a fellow human being. Let us identify with those overwhelming human feelings. To do so I think it is more helpful if we imagine it through the eyes of someone watching a loved one in pain. Just for a moment, imagine that it is not Jesus but your own human father or mother in agony on the cross. See the pain, suffering and anguish. It is your father or mother and you cannot bear to see it anymore. But feel the pain and know that pain. Their pain is so overwhelming to watch that it nearly pierces your own flesh. Our reaction is almost universal – we want to stop the suffering. Yes, the first thing we want to do is relieve it.

But this human reality exists among us here and now. It is hard to watch as your young son or daughter suffers from cancer, desperately holding onto life by a string. It is hard to watch as your mother or father suffers in their old age from dementia or other debilitating illnesses. It is hard to watch as your friend or family member suffers from depression when they cannot find a job or recover from a broken relationship. Yes, it is hard to watch as others suffer or as we suffer. In every community there are people in pain and suffering, in their agony of the garden of their lives, or on the cross experiencing pain beyond imagination. We have in our community such a mother and father watching their son. We have such a son and daughter watching their father. We have such family members watching their friends.

However, the message that Jesus Christ gives us through his passion is not so much about pain and death, as much as it is about the hope in and beyond the suffering. God will never abandon us. God will always be there, especially in the midst of the pain. So, if we are watching a loved one in pain or suffering or are ourselves in pain, know that God will never abandon us. God is always there.

Do We Understand?

When I was a child, I used to play rugby very competitively. We would have three or four training sessions a week with a game on the weekend. Every time I came back from practice or a game I would have filthy dirty gear. It rains a lot in Ireland and most of the time our rugby gear would be covered in heavy black mud. When my brothers and I arrived home, (remember there were ten boys in my family), it was our custom to take all the dirty gear out of the gear bag and throw it on the floor outside the kitchen.

From there, my mom would sort the gear by colour and wash them. I never really took much notice of the routine my mother had. All I knew was the next night I had shiny white gear for the next game. What I did not know until much later in life was how difficult it was to wash the white clothes. She would soak them in a bucket to get the heavy dirt off, then she would wash them twice or three times, then she would dry and fold them, ready for use again. Imagine that much laundry day after day. I had no idea until I saw what she did and really watched her. I did not understand what she had done for me for all those years!

There are many people in our lives who have served us and we do not understand what they have done for us. Maybe it is our parents, who have washed our laundry or cooked our meals. Maybe it is our spouses, who have worked hard to give us what we have. Maybe it is our children, who now take care of us in our old age. Or maybe it is a friend, who served us in our time of need. Do we understand what they have done for us?

Jesus in today's gospel gives us a profound model of service for one another. He, the master and the Lord, gets down on his knees to wash the filthy feet of his friends and disciples. He says this is what we must do for one another. He asks us if we understand what he has done for us.

To be honest with ourselves, we need to take some serious time during Holy Week praying and reflect on that message: Do we know what God has done for us? We need to examine our lives and recognise how blessed we are by God: the gift of our health, our families, our friends, and our freedom. We are called to recognise how much we have been gifted and then to follow

Christ's example of service to others. We are called to bend low in service of others. Maybe it is our parents, children, or friends but it could be someone else in need this week. May we understand what he has done for us and do the same for others.

Only One Move – Love

A ten-year-old boy lost his left arm in a devastating auto accident. Once he had recovered, he began judo lessons. His teacher – his *sensei* – was an old Japanese master. The boy was doing very well in his lessons. But he could not understand why, after three months of dedicated lessons, the master had only taught him one move. '*Sensei*,' the boy finally asked, 'shouldn't I be learning more moves?'

'This is the only move you know,'the sensei replied, 'but this is the only move you will ever need to know.' Not quite understanding, but believing in his teacher, the boy continued training and mastering his one move.

Several months later, the *sensei* took the boy to his first tournament. The boy, to his surprise, easily won his first and second matches. The third match proved a little more difficult, but after some time, his opponent became impatient and charged; the boy deftly employed his one move and won the match. Still amazed at his success, the boy was now in the finals.

This time his opponent was bigger, stronger, and more experienced. The boy appeared to be overmatched. Concerned that the boy might get hurt, the referee called a time-out. He was about to stop the match when the *sensei* intervened. 'No, let them continue,' the *sensei* insisted.

Soon after the match resumed, the boy's opponent made a critical mistake: he dropped his guard and the boy used his move to pin him. The boy won the match and the tournament.

On the way home, the boy and the *sensei* reviewed every move of every match. The boy finally summoned up enough courage to ask what was really on his mind. '*Sensei*, how did I win the tournament with only one move?' 'You won for two reasons,' the *sensei* answered. 'First, you've almost mastered one of the most difficult moves in all of judo. And second, the only known defence for that move is for your opponent to grab your left arm, and you don't have one!'[1]

We all have crosses to bear. We often think of our crosses as burdens, something or someone that demands so much of our

---

1. *Connections* (Mediaworks, Londonderry, NH: March, 2006) p 2

energy and time. We wonder why God gave us such a cross, or what would life be like without such a burden. Yet, it is the cross that gives us an opportunity to define ourselves. The cross can be our greatest strength if only we can see things differently.

In today's gospel, we hear the passion of Christ and we hear how Jesus bears his cross. He had only one move: it was to love, and there is no defence against it, not even death itself. Jesus chose to love others right to the very end. Jesus perfected this loving and mastered it. He was love itself made human. So we are called to love, too.

If we are to overcome our struggles or pains then we need to learn the only move we will ever need – love. It is in loving that our crosses become more than crosses; they become the reality of our lives of faith. It is in loving that our crosses become our strengths.

That is all fine to say but some of our crosses are very heavy. Maybe we have significant struggles at school with learning disabilities, or lack of skills, or friends. Maybe it is at the office as we struggle to enjoy the work we do or to get along with the other people in the office. Maybe it is in our homes as we struggle with the cross of poor relationships with our spouse, children, or parents. Maybe we are caring for them in their sickness or dying days. Maybe we have already experienced the loss of a loved one to death and the cross of pain is still raw on our shoulders. Maybe we have struggled with our own personality peculiarity all our lives and we cannot seem to overcome it. We have tried so hard to carry our crosses but never seem to overcome the sheer weight of it and now we are tired of it.

Today the Lord says to us that through our crosses he will make us strong and successful. Today, we need to learn that one move. That one move we need to practice over and over again, every day, every week, every month, and every year till we perfect it for the tournament of life itself. Some days we meet bigger and stronger opponents than us but with love we can overcome any scenario. It is love that overcomes the cross for Christ and it will be love that overcomes the cross for us.

Today, as we come forward to venerate the cross, may we call to mind the current cross we carry; as we kiss the wood of the cross, may we remember that it is Christ's example of love that will help us to be strengthened through our crosses. We do not overcome our cross, but we can gain victory by loving despite the cross. Today and every day, may we practice that one move we need – that only move we will ever need – loving others.

Book of Possibilities

In a recent blockbuster movie called *Last Holiday*, Queen Latifah plays the role of a shy, New Orleans cookware salesclerk called Georgia Byrd. After hitting her head in a store accident and visiting the store doctor, she is led to believe that she has less than a month to live. It's time to give her life a serious makeover. All of her life she has kept a book of possibilities. This is where she keeps all the recipes of meals she never ate but wanted to, all the vacations she dreamt of but never took, and all the men she wanted to date but never asked – it was her life of possibilities. Now she starts to live from that book. Georgia jets off on a dream vacation to the 'Grandhotel Pupp' near Prague, to live like there is no tomorrow! There, thinking she has nothing to lose, Georgia undergoes a transformation; a transformation that affects everyone around her. Georgia's new, uninhibited personality shakes up staff and guests alike, including a venerated chef (Gerard Depardieu) as well as a retail magnate (Timothy Hutton), who becomes convinced she's a rival intent on sabotaging his business plans. From snowy slopes, to spectacular spas, delectable dinners, to midnight balls, Georgia lives it up for the next few weeks only to discover that she was misdiagnosed. But, now that she was transformed, she cannot go back to her old self.

The candidates and the elect tonight have been on a journey, a serious makeover, if you would. They open the book of possibilities and will start to live from that book of life in Christ. They are about to be transformed in baptism or confirmation, and there is no going back to the old way of life. We, too, have walked with them on their journey through Lent and we recall tonight our own baptism and the call to follow Christ. Tonight, there is no misdiagnosis – tonight, the elect and candidates will be transformed, transformed into a new being in Christ!

Through the many readings, we hear the story of humanity and how we have taken our lives for granted. The people of Israel and the first Christians got distracted from God's way of life for them. We, too, often get distracted from God's way of life for us, and we have often turned away and sinned. We take for granted the many gifts we have in our lives: our children, our parents, our families, our friends, our school or work, our health, our country, our freedom. But tonight we promise to transform ourselves anew and promise to live life more fully; not just possibilities but realities.

In the gospel tonight, we hear how Mary and the disciples arrive at the tomb to find the stone rolled away. Although they did not believe at first, they came to believe and understand that Christ had risen from the dead. The stone was not rolled away for the sake of the person inside, rather it was rolled away for the sake of the people outside. It was rolled away for the disciples' sakes and ours. Jesus did not need the stone to roll away for his resurrection. That was done for the disciples and for us. We are called to respond like the beloved disciple: to see and believe even though we do not fully understand.

Tonight, may we truly see with eyes of faith and choose to believe that Christ is risen from the dead and lives in you and me. We do not need to be misdiagnosed with an early death; we can choose to live fully today. We can choose to live fully in the Spirit of Christ. May we shake off our weaknesses and doubts, and live fully as a disciple in Christ. We need to grasp life for all it's worth.

There is a great scene towards the end of the movie where Georgia looks in the mirror; all dressed up, before she attends the New Year's Eve dinner, thinking it was her last night out, and says to herself, 'You didn't get everything you wanted, but you didn't do so bad. Next time, we do things differently. We will laugh more, live more, love more, see the world. We won't be so afraid!'

We need to take out our book of possibilities and live as a child of God. As we renew our baptismal promises in a few minutes, I suggest we look into the waters of the baptismal font and renew our promise to God and to ourselves. We didn't get everything we ever wanted, but from here on, we will do things differently. We will laugh a little more, live a little more, love a little more, and we won't be afraid to live life more fully. We will live more in the Spirit by grasping life for all its worth, and laugh more, live more, love more as Christ is alive within us.

Know God: Obey the Rules

If I were to say to you that 'I am a good driver' what sort of proof would you require to believe me? Some might say they want to see my driver's licence. Others might ask for proof that I actually have experience driving a car. Still others might want to ensure that I have no speeding tickets.

Having a driver's licence is another way of checking if I know the rules. But does 'having a licence' make a person a good driver? We all know that is not true! Knowing the rules and obeying the rules are two different things. In fact, there are a lot of bad drivers with licences and I am sure most of us have experienced one or two in our day.

I am just back from Atlanta and I can tell you California does not have the corner on the market of bad drivers. Neither are we much better than anyone else. Just the other week, I was driving in the second lane, when the car in the fast lane decides they need to exit, which is only two hundred yards away. So they cut across four lanes of traffic and make the exit. All of the surrounding cars slammed on our brakes and barely missed the maneuvering car. Luckily, we avoided each other in the process. We all wondered, 'What on earth was that the person thinking? Did they not know the rules of the road?' I am not going to tell you what ethnic group or gender because no ethnic group or gender have the corner on the market of bad drivers either.

What makes a good driver? A good driver is someone who drives safely, courteously, and has no tickets. Put another way, a person who obeys the rules of the road. For if one obeys the rules of the road then one is driving safely, courteously, and will avoid tickets. But they still need to actually drive and have the experience of driving a car itself. For without driving a car at some stage, all the knowledge of the rules or the willingness to obey the rules, will not make you a good driver. We need to know the rules, obey them, and practise them.

Today, we celebrate the resurrection of Christ and people all over the world come to church to recognise and celebrate Christ's central message: love God and love one another as yourself. This is his one commandment, his one rule. It is not enough to simply 'know' the commandments, we need to live and obey the commandments. We need to know, obey, and practice the commandments in our every day lives and not just intellectually 'know' them. That makes a lot of sense when we hear it and it is quite simple to understand. Yet, it is not so easy to do.

Just like the driver who knows all the rules of the road, obeying them all the time when actually driving is not so easy. Who among us has always, and everywhere, driven according to the rules of the road – without speeding or other common violations? Yes, we know the rules of the road but we sometimes fail to adhere to all the rules all the time. The rules are simple but always obeying them is not so easy. The same is true of our discipleship: the commandments are simple but obeying them all the time is not so easy. The rule is simple: to love others, to serve others, and forgive others; but that is not easy to do that all the time.

In our radically individualistic society, we often think that our sins are our own business, just between God and me. But is that true? Don't our actions have an impact on those around us? Just like the bad driver has a negative effect on those who are around them (sometimes fatally so), when we sin, we too have a negative effect on those closest to us. For example, when we lie to our children, parents or friends, we lose their trust in us and erode our relationship with them. When we get angry or say something wrong, our children watch and remember those words and actions, repeating them at the most inconvenient times. When we are unkind to people by what we say and do; then others rightly ask how we can do such a thing and call ourselves Christian? Where is the Christian behaviour?

This simple command of knowing our God by obeying his commandment is true, but not easy to live. That is why we come here each week: to receive nourishment, encouragement, and strength. We know that we fail in small ways each week, but we come seeking renewal and refreshment. Jesus promises to give us his very self here at this Eucharist so we can be renewed for the next week to live this command. Each week we come to the table to be encouraged by one another and obey his command to love, serve, and forgive others.

Today as we celebrate the resurrection of the Lord, may we truly live it in our lives. As we leave here, getting into our cars to drive, may we be aware of the way we drive and obey the rules. May we also obey the rules of our Christian discipleship by loving, serving, and forgiving others in our daily lives.

Jesus, the Spiritual GPS

Since I arrived in Atlanta from San Jose, I have been staying with Joe & Roseanne DiBenedetto. They have been very generous and kind, allowing me to use one of their cars. It has this really cool Global Positioning System (GPS) that will navigate you to or from anywhere. Have you ever seen one? You just type in your destination and this sweet voice comes on telling you where to go. 'In 400 yards take a left turn and then a right turn.' It is a woman's voice (the DiBenedetto's call her Gladys). She's very calming to a distressed driver. If you take a wrong turn or miss a turn, she will recalculate and give you new directions. No matter what, she will guide you to your destination. And when you reach your final destination, she says, 'You have arrived at your final destination. Good bye.'

There is one feature that is particularly cool: it is a little 'house' icon at the bottom of the screen – these are the directions home – and when you press it, she will give you directions to get home. You will never be lost with this GPS. Still, you need to listen to her instructions to get home. If I ignore the instructions, I will not get anywhere. I still need to listen carefully as the instructions can be detailed and important. Actually, when driving to Atlanta yesterday, I had the satellite radio on, listening to 70s music, and I had the volume way up, so when Gladys came on I could hardly hear, 'Take the next exit in 2 miles, exit 168.' I almost missed the exit because I was distracted listening to the radio. Yes, it is great to have a GPS; but if we are to get where we want to go then we have to listen to the instructions.

We have a spiritual GPS with Jesus. 'He is the way, the truth and the life.' Jesus is always guiding us home to the Father. No matter how far we stray or how many wrong turns we take, Jesus is always giving us a new route home to the Father. However, just like the GPS of the DiBenedetto's car, there are two things we need to do: we need to be able to hear the directions given to us and heed the directions and commands.

In the gospel today, we hear how the disciples were in the upper room hidden in fear. They all doubted the message of the Messiah Jesus and were unsure of what to do next. Here are the disciples, the friends of Jesus – these guys really knew him –

and yet they still doubted what they had heard. They allowed the voices of doubt and fear to creep into their hearts and they could no longer hear the guiding voice of their Messiah. Thomas is the epitome of that doubt and fear. He would not believe even when his friends believed. He demanded to see and touch the Lord for himself.

Often in our lives there are so many distractions that we cannot hear the gentle guiding voice of Jesus. Voices of doubt and fear creep into our hearts and we no longer hear the voice of Jesus; we no longer hear the Lord's commands. Like the radio in the car while I was driving to Atlanta I could not hear the voice of the GPS system. We often have so many things going on in our lives that we cannot hear the voice of Jesus. We have so much stuff going on; we have no time to listen to Jesus in prayer. Whether it be at work, or at school, or at home, whether it be playing, or watching sports; whether it be taking care of home chores or office duties; whether it be something painful that is happening to us; whether we are caught up in our own success; we do not take the time for prayer and so are lost in our way through life. We can no longer hear the instructions of Jesus.

Maybe Jesus is talking to us through our family or friends and we need to take the time to listen to the instructions. Maybe we can take the time to listen to our child who has come home from a tough day at school, because school has gone bad, or they were teased or something. Maybe we can listen to our spouse who has come in from a ridiculously difficult day at work or has been at home all day with the sick kids. Maybe we can tend to the needs of our elderly parents and listen to them in their time of need in old age, giving back to them after so many years of loving us. Maybe there is some friend who has tried to talk to us in their time of need.

The second part of this spiritual GPS is following his instructions so we can make it home. Today's second reading from the first Letter of John tells us that we are begotten by God when we love God, when we love others and obey his commandments. 'His commands are not burdensome.' Yes, to listen and obey Jesus' commandments is to do the will of the Father and it will take us home.

Here is the real kicker today. The apostles took his commandments and lived them completely. In today's first reading from the Acts of the Apostles, we hear about the struggles they had in living this reality. We hear how all the disciples sold everything they had and brought the proceeds to the apostles so they could distribute according to each other's needs. You will notice that they distribute according to *need*, not *want*.

I am not suggesting that you all go out, sell everything and bring the proceeds to the church. We know that is not a reality. However, we ought to ask ourselves: how do we spend our selves? I do not mean our money (although that could be a valuable exercise too). I mean, how do we spend our time?

I acknowledge it is great that so many come to church on Sunday for this prayer and worship of God. However, we come here for one hour a week but we live the reality of our discipleship in the other 167 hours of the week outside of this building and in our daily lives. It is in our every day life that we are called to live Jesus' commandment to love one another. We need to ask how do we spend our selves this week and do we obey the commandments of Jesus. This week may we listen to the voice of Jesus in our child, spouse, parent, or friend and be ready to act on the instructions we hear. This week, may we listen carefully to the instructions we hear from Jesus, our spiritual GPS, and obey his command to love one another.

We Become What We Receive

Over this last week I had the opportunity to visit some parish families who are dealing with some health problems. Actually, they are struggling with different forms of cancer. One family's child, who is only four years old, has a large, cancerous tumour. The other family's mother has cancer on top of another major illness which significantly complicates the treatment process. Both families are strong believers and faith-filled people, coming to church regularly and helping people at any given opportunity. They are really struggling to see God in the midst of all of this pain. Both families are desperately seeking to understand how God could let this happen to them. Some of their friends suggest that God is putting them to the test. 'The cancer is God's way of testing their faith,' their friends say. Other friends rather cruelly suggest that if they had enough faith then they would not be ill and the cancer would leave. Still other friends suggest there could not be a God at all if God could let this happen to them.

I suggest that God is there in the midst of all our pain. God does not abandon us in any way but is with us always, helping us to endure the pain, understand the illness and options, and cope with the consequences. I do not believe our God would send us cancer as a 'test' as if to play with us as puppets. God loves us too much to send us pain as a test. What parent among us would burn our child's hand so we can teach them how to use a bandage or ointment! No, our God does not send us 'cancer' as a test of faith. However, it is true that our faith will be put to the test as a result of the pain we endure. God does not send us a trial just to test the quality of our faith. Nor does the amount of illness depend on the amount of faith. If that were the case, then no believer would ever get sick. If that were the case, then Christ would not have had to die on the cross, for he had enough faith for all of humanity. Nor do I believe there is no God. I have too much evidence to the contrary!

No! God is with us, especially in those painful and dark times. When the dark clouds veil the skies of our lives, God is still by our side. No matter how blind we are to his presence, he is always there and he will never abandon us, ever. Sometimes the pain of our lives is so much we cannot see or hear him. But believe me when I say that God is there in the midst of the storm. Yes, he will be there after the storm in the sunshine again but he is also here now in the rain and clouds. He is with us in the thunder of pain that frightens us. He is always there!

In today's gospel, the disciples are leaving Jerusalem because they are disappointed, saddened, and maybe even angry. They had followed Jesus for a number of years because they thought he was the one to set them free. And now he is dead and they do not understand how God could do this to them. Right in the midst of their pain and questioning, Jesus comes to them and is with them. He breaks open the scriptures so they can understand and their eyes were opened in the breaking of the bread. It is often disconcerting to think that as soon as they realise it was Christ himself, he vanishes from their sight. Where does he go, we think? He does not disappear but rather they now *become* Christ. In the breaking of the bread, they become what they receive – the Body of Christ. Every Sunday we come to this table, we break open the scriptures, and then we break the bread in much the same way these disciples did. And we become what we receive – the Body of Christ. We are called to go forth from here to be that Body of Christ to others. We are called to be the bright sun in the dark clouds of others' lives.

Right now, if you are experiencing dark clouds in your life whether medical problems of cancer or relationship problems or any of the other pains and troubles that affect our lives, believe me when I say that God is always by our side. God is in the storm, in the rain, and in the clouds. If you do not see him, then believe me when I say he is still there. Just believe that he is there.

And if we do not have dark clouds in our life right now and the sun is shining brightly, then maybe we need to be that bright light in others' lives. We need to realise it is our turn to help others who are experiencing dark clouds in their lives. As we are dismissed from here today, know that it is our role to be Christ to others. Today, as we come to the table and break the bread and receive, may we know that we become what we receive — the Body of Christ.

Know the Voice of the Shepherd

Not too long ago an old friend of mine called me out of the blue. The conversation went something like this: 'Hey, Brendan. It's Gerry. How are you doing? How are things going in the parish? How is priesthood treating you?' I answered, 'Great, just wonderful! How are things with you?' struggling to recognise the voice with whom I was speaking. I vaguely recognised the voice but I could not place a face. I knew the name, Gerry, but for the life of me, I could not put it together with a face. Which Gerry was it? I knew so many! The conversation became very personal and it was clear that he knew me well but I still could not recognise the voice. I let the conversation go a while more and eventually interrupted, 'I'm sorry who is this again?' 'It's Gerry!' he said curtly. Still not recognising the voice, I asked, 'Gerry who?' 'Gerry O'Connor. Can't you recognise my voice?' 'Oh my! Gerry O'Connor! I have not talked with you in at least four years. No, I did not recognise your voice. It's been so long. You sound different. How are you doing?' And so we caught up with times past.

Yes, we do recognise the voices of our friends, families, co-workers, and maybe even famous people. But the assumption is that we spend a lot of time with them – people with whom live, work, or listen. We only need a few words from them and we know who it is. For example, I talk with my brother almost every day and I only need to hear his voice to know that it is indeed him on the phone. A better example is when he and his wife are chatting on the cell phone. There are only a few words in the conversation and the communication is done. They know each other by their voices. Can you imagine not talking with an acquaintance for four years and then one day hearing their voice? Yes, they would seem like strangers!

Well, in today's gospel we hear John's version of the Good Shepherd and how the sheep recognise the shepherd's voice and follow him. They will run away from a stranger's voice because they do not know him. But they recognise the shepherd's voice because they are always with him. The shepherd goes ahead of the flock and calls them and they will follow. We are called to recognise the voice of our Good Shepherd and to always follow him. The responsorial Psalm we sung today puts it well: we follow the Lord because he is always with us. We follow the Lord because he is our friend. We want to follow him always.

If, however, we do not spend time with our Lord then we will not recognise his voice when he calls. I know of no other way to learn the sound of his voice than to spend quality time in prayer each day. I know I say this a lot, but we need to find time each day to pray. If only ten minutes or even five minutes, we need to pray daily. We are called to find some quiet space in our life and listen to the Lord. I challenge you again to spend ten minutes each day in prayer, reading the Bible, learning the sound of his voice, so when he calls us we will follow. As the opening prayer says, 'Attune our minds to the sound of your voice; lead our steps in the path that he has shown.'

Let us listen again to the words of the song we just sang: 'Because the Lord is my shepherd, I have everything I need. He lets me rest in the meadow and leads me to the quiet streams. He restores my soul and he leads me in the paths that are right. Lord, you are my shepherd, you are my friend. I want to follow you always, just to follow my friend.'[1]

---

1. Christopher Walker, 'Because the Lord is My Shepherd' (OCP Publications: Portland, Oregon, 1985).

Cairns For Society: Living Stones of Christ

As many of you know, I love to hike mountains, especially those tall mountains over 14,000 feet in Colorado. Success in climbing these mountains is not only about fitness. It is also about following the right path up the mountain. These trails are not well worn as only a few people climb them. So it is important that we watch the markers carefully. While climbing these major mountains, one will reach a point where several little trails branch off. They all bring you to a different place. Some trails are the correct ones and bring you up to the top. Other trails bring you over the edge of the mountain where only deer can walk! The only way one knows the difference is markers called 'cairns'. Cairns are piles of rocks and stones stacked to form a sort of pyramid. These cairns are made by hikers who have gone here before and know the difficult path ahead. They stack rocks on top of one another to point to the correct path. These cairns can be small, with just a few stones stacked on top of each other or they can be huge ones made of hundreds of stones.

One day, I remember climbing a particularly steep mountain and we came to the intersection of trails as usual. This time all the trails looked equally worn and we could not see any cairns. Then our eyes caught the top stone of what appeared to be a cairn. It was very small and far off in the distance. We took the risk and headed for it. When we eventually arrived at its location, it was huge. It was at least six-feet high and six-feet wide! But from down below, it was just barely visible. Yet, it was the only marker to be seen. It was the only way for us to know the way!

In today's gospel, Jesus tells the disciples that he is 'the way'. And in the second reading from the Letter of Peter, we are told that we are the living stones of the church with Christ as the keystone or capstone. Put another way, we point the way to God by being the church. Or we could say, we are the 'cairn for society' that points to Christ and his way to God. Every time we gather as a group of believers, the people of God, then we are showing people the way to Christ. Every time we gather, our actions tell others how Christians are called to be in this world. Whether we gather around for coffee at work, or in the neighbourhood for company, or in the schoolyard to play, all our actions tell others how we, Christians, are called to act. If we gossip about others or are mean to them in some way, then it tells others that is who we are. If we are kind to others in word and deed, then it tells others that is who we are. We have a choice each day and each week!

When we gather around this table each Sunday, we come together to pray and worship as a community. But it is in the world of our daily lives that we live out this liturgy as individuals. It is in our homes, offices, and schools that we show the world what we learn from being here at church. It is outside of this church building that we are 'church – the people of God.' Yes, we are the 'living stones' that is the church.

This week, we leave this church building knowing that we become the living church. We become the living stones of Christ in the world and every action is noted by those around us as a pointer to God. Every word we say and every action we take is a marker – a cairn to society on a difficult road of life, that keeps ourselves, and others, on the way of Christ. If we fall back, we will recognise the path again. And for those who do not know the way at all, we proclaim, by our actions, the way of Christ. Today and this week, whether we are at work in the office, or at home or school with our family and friends, or in the neighbourhood with other community members, we are called to remember that all our actions are markers for others. May we point the way to Christ, for we are the living stones of the church of Christ.

6th Sunday of Easter
Acts 8:5-8, 14-17; Psalm 66; 1 Peter 3:15-18; John 14:15-21

Real Promises, Not Piecrust Promises

In the movie *Mary Poppins*, the two children, Jane and Michael Banks, jump into bed after spending their first day with their amazing, new nanny. They were so excited with her, little Jane asks her, 'Mary, you won't ever leave us, will you?' Michael wanting more reassurance adds, 'Will you promise to stay forever, if we promise to be good?' Mary smiles at her two little friends and replies, 'Look, that's just a piecrust promise. Easy to make and easy to break!'[1]

That is so true, some promises are easy to make and easy to break. Because we do not think much about the 'making' of them, we do not think much about the 'breaking' of them. An example, for some of our children, is when we say to our parent, 'Mom, I promise to be good if I can have the ice cream.' We get the ice cream and forget about being good. Or we say to another boy or girl at school, 'I promise to be your friend forever if you let me play with your toys.' When we are finished playing with their toys, we are done being friends too! We adults are not much better at these promises: When we leave to go to college, we promise our parents, 'I promise to write or call often,' but we quickly forget after meeting some new friends. Or the proverbial, 'Let's do lunch, some day!' when we have no intention of meeting for lunch. The lists could go on for both children and adults. Yes, we make a lot of piecrust promises – easy to make and easy to break.

Now I would like to speak to the boys and girls who are making their First Eucharist/Communion today. Many years ago your parents made some promises, and they were not piecrust promises, they were real promises. When you were young, your parents had you baptised. Back then, they promised to train you in the practice of the faith, helping you to keep the commandments as Christ has taught us, by loving God and our neighbours. And so today, we gather around this table to celebrate your First Eucharist and they are fulfilling their real promise to practice their faith.

---

1. Patricia Datchuck Sanchez, 'Celebration: An Ecumenical Worship Resource,' (Kansas City, Montana: National Catholic Reporter Company, Inc, May 2005).

In today's gospel, we hear Jesus give his disciples, and us, a real promise that will last for all of eternity. He promised not leave us alone in this world but to be with us forever. He said he would give us a special gift from the Father – the gift of the Holy Spirit. He called him 'the Advocate' because the Holy Spirit is not a passive gift, but an active one who encourages us to do good, encourages us to love others, and pushes us forward when we are down. Even more importantly, he puts this Advocate or Holy Spirit right in our hearts to dwell within us. So, not only is Christ with us forever but he is *within* us forever. That is no piecrust promise but a real promise. Today, and every Sunday, we celebrate that real promise.

In return he asks us to make a real promise. He asks us to love one another as he has loved us. Now, we adults know how difficult this promise is to make and how difficult it really is to keep. We come back here to this table each Sunday, to receive the strength to keep the promise that Jesus asks of us. We do not come here each week because we have to, but because we want to, and need to, for nourishment and strength. We know that each week we will fail in some way to love others and so we come back here each Sunday to ask God's forgiveness and courage to try harder. We encourage you to come back here each week too. We, the community, give you this real promise as you continue your journey of faith.

And today as we celebrate this special occasion for you, as you receive your First Eucharist/Communion, your first opportunity to get this nourishment from this table, Jesus asks us to love one another. For you, boys and girls, that means that we love our little brother or sister even when they act weird or strange, we love our mother or father even when they do not give us what we want; we love our grandparents even when they get old and needy; we love our school classmates even when they are not nice to us. For all of us, it means loving even when it is not easy. Jesus promises to be within us, always, through the Holy Spirit. That is a real promise and not a piecrust promise. And in return, we promise to love others always. That is a real promise, not a piecrust promise.

Open the Eyes of Your Heart

Boys and girls receiving your First Eucharist/Communion, I have a question for you today. What does the word 'invisible' mean? That's right, not able to see something. So 'visible' then means being able to see something, right? Examples of something visible are the things around us, such as our car, our houses, this chair, table, our hands, our feet, and even this church building we are in today. An example of something invisible is the air or wind, the love we share as family members, faith, Jesus, and the Spirit of God. Yet each of these things, both visible and invisible, are real and we believe they exist.

We believe visible things exist because we can see them with our eyes and we can physically touch them as well. Invisible things are different. We cannot see them in the same way although we know them to be real. We know that air exists because it touches us. The same is true of the love of our parents. We know that our parents' love exists because it moves our hearts and souls. The same is true of the Spirit of God. We know that it exists when it touches us. We do see invisible things but not with our physical, ordinary eyes but with the eyes of our hearts.

That is the expression used in the Letter to the Ephesians today. It says, 'May the eyes of your hearts be enlightened, that you may know what is the hope that belongs to his call, what are the riches of glory in his inheritance among the holy ones, and what is the surpassing greatness of his power for us who believe …' Yes, the Lord wants us to open the eyes of our hearts so that we can become enlightened to his grace. The Lord wants us to see the 'invisible' in our lives. The Lord wants us to see the love he gives us through our parents' love. The Lord wants us to see his invisible presence in our world. To help us do so, he gives us an invisible gift called the Holy Spirit. He puts this Holy Spirit inside our hearts so that we can keep the eyes of our heart wide open. That is the promise Jesus gives his disciples in today's gospel. God, who was visible for a limited time and place in Jesus, now becomes invisible again with the Ascension. He does not abandon us, but becomes our hope. He wants us to keep the eyes of our hearts open.

It is not always so easy to keep those eyes open. In the same way, we close our physical eyes when we don't want to see the mess we leave our bedroom or the kitchen. It is sometimes easier to close our hearts' eyes and pretend we don't see those invisible gifts. But we are called to open wide the eyes of our hearts. We adults, know it is hard to keep those eyes open and so we come back to this table each week on Sunday to help in that challenge. Each week we receive the Body and Blood of Christ and it helps to open the eyes of our hearts. So, we encourage you boys and girls to come back every week for this eye-opening gift.

Boys and girls, today you will receive your first Eucharist and you will experience for the first time what this means. Today, we see the bread and wine with our physical eyes because it is visible. But with our heart's eyes we see the Body and Blood of Christ. You will receive the Body of Christ but you will also become what you receive – the Body of Christ to others. Today and this week, may we allow the gift of the Holy Spirit within us to see with our heart's eyes and recognise the Risen Lord in this bread and wine and so become what we receive.

Source of Life

During these last few weeks, I have had the opportunity to do some miscellaneous tasks around the house. One of the projects involved drilling some holes and I needed to use the cordless power drill. So I grabbed it and went to use it but there was no power. I pulled out the battery and replaced it with the spare battery. I plugged in the new battery only to find no power again. I was at a loss. I mean, what does a man do without his power tool! It is every man's faithful companion. I wanted to drill a hole but what do I do without the drill?

Then I remembered back to my childhood days when my father did not have a power drill. He used a tool called an awl; it's a sharp pointed tool that allows you to bore a small hole. Surprisingly, I had an awl and used it to push a few holes. Well afterwards my arm and shoulder were hurting me badly; I was exhausted after just a few small holes. One forgets the power behind those power drills. Just a few holes with an awl and I was done for the day! I remember when my father got his first power drill; it was old Black & Decker drill, metallic blue with a really short cord. It was easy to remember where the power came from, as it always had to be plugged into the power outlet. There was no such thing as a cordless drill back then. One was always tethered by these extension cords that seem to get all tangled up at every use.

I think the same is true for our lives as Christians. We are like these cordless power drills; very independent and capable of lots of tasks. The danger is that we forget we are not our own power source. Our real source and power is from God through Christ. This becomes evident when we have to do things for ourselves in those times when we doubt and our faith falters. Then we think, 'How did we ever survive without faith?' When we go through those difficult times in our lives, we realise how much we have taken for granted our source of strength and power in Christ that dwells within us.

Even Jesus realised that his source of strength was his relationship with his Father in heaven. He knew he needed to pray often to renew himself and his disciples in his Father's love. In today's gospel, we hear Jesus pray to his Father for his friends and disciples; that they may remain strong and focused on glorifying the Father. Indeed, the disciples got that message as we hear in the first readings from the Acts of the Apostles. We read how they gathered in prayer in the upper room; they needed to recharge themselves after their journey from Jerusalem.

For those of us who have been through difficult times, we know how important our faith really is. Indeed, we wonder how we could have managed without it. That is the very thing we celebrate when we come to this table to receive the bread and wine now made into the Body and Blood of Christ. We receive this true nourishment from God. We come to receive that nourishment in order to be strengthened for the journey of the week ahead.

Sometimes, when we come here and we do not make it back for a few weeks, our batteries run low. Other times we don't really notice our battery level because we do not really use the strength within us at all. We often plod along in life, not doing much of anything. We do little harm to anyone; but we do little good to anyone either. If we are really interested in living life to the fullest, then we will find our batteries are drained in a day because we are fully alive in Christ. Not only do we use our batteries, but we use the spare, too. Then we will need to recharge during the week. That is what we are called to do: to live life to the fullest, to utilise our every ounce of strength in service to others, to be alive fully in the Spirit. When we come here each Sunday, this is the beginning of our week. We do not stop here, but rather begin here.

It is not enough to just come here on Sundays. Yes, we come here to recharge ourselves as a community and as individuals but we need to also find a place to recharge our batteries during the week. We need to find some time with the Lord every single day. I know that, especially for so many young families, life is very hectic all the time. There is so much stuff coming at us, especially now, with getting ready for the beginning of another school year. But I do not know anyone who is not busy. It seems that even in retirement, we are busy with something. All of us are challenged to find that time to pray. All of us are challenged to recharge our own batteries.

And where does that prayer start? I suggest we start with a prayer of thanksgiving and praise. We start by saying: thank you God, for the gift of our children even though they can be unruly at times; thank you for the gift of our parents even though they can be needy now in their old age; thank you for the gift of my health and I'm able to get up in the morning; thank you for the gift of our very lives.

This week, as we leave here with our fully charged batteries, may we take the time to pray each day as individuals to continue to recharge our batteries during the week. It will not happen on its own; we have to deliberately choose to spend that time with the Lord.

The Incredible Christian Family

In the movie, *The Incredibles*, the story is told of a family who possess 'incredible' or superhuman talents. There is Mr Incredible who has superhuman upper body strength; Elastigirl who can stretch into any shape; Dash who can run super fast; Violet who can create a force field; and the baby who has an unusual set of talents that I will not share because it will spoil the great ending to the movie. The plot starts with Mr Incredible working for the government, busy saving people at a moment's notice. He and his family are put into the Federal protection programme because there are a superabundant number of lawsuits pending, from people who did not want to be saved.

In this hidden life, the Incredible family pretend not to have these incredible gifts and find it hard to blend in. Each member in their own way, find ways to express their talent for good. Mr Incredible finds it all too much and he takes an opportunity, when presented, to go back to his real life of using his superhuman powers for the good of others. This time, however, he is up against a force greater than himself and needs the help of other superhumans. Eventually, his family comes and saves him. When each of them tries to fight the evil on his own they are defeated. But when they bind together, their unity of family love defeats the evil Syndrome, with his poisonous envy of Mr Incredible.[1]

It is a great movie if you haven't seen it; it serves as an allegory of our lives. Just like the Incredible family, we all have different gifts. While we may not have superhuman talents we all have gifts of some sort. If we pretend we do not have these gifts, then we cannot live life fully. We will feel we are missing something, and we will. If we use these gifts for just our own good, we will eventually feel out of sync. If we envy the gifts of others and seek revenge, like Syndrome, then we will destroy ourselves as well as the other person. Instead, we are called to recognise the gifts of ourselves first, and then use those gifts for the sake of the

1. Inspired by comments in 'Homily Helps,' (St Anthony Messenger Press: Cincinnati, OH, May, 2005) and Patricia Datchuck Sanchez, 'Celebration: An Ecumenical Worship Resource,' (Kansas City, Montana: National Catholic Reporter Company, Inc, May 2005).

common good. If we bind together as a family, our love will have superhuman qualities.

In today's second reading from Paul's letter to the Corinthians, we hear the passage dealing with the different gifts of the community. In this section, Paul assures us, in baptism all share in the same Spirit. All parts of the body, which is the church, have different and diverse gifts but all rely on each other for the good of the whole body. Yes, the day we were baptised, we were given a share in the Spirit that enables us to see that the gifts given to us are used for the good of all. We are all gifted, not just the leaders of the community. Nor have these gifts been given solely for our personal enlightenment or pleasure, but for the common good of all. The analogy of the human body that Paul gives is a powerful metaphor of the interdependence of each part. For example, the ear cannot be the eye nor can the foot be the kidney. Each part of the body relies on the other parts to do its job.

So it is for each of us. We are called to recognise our own unique contribution to the whole. Each of us has gifts of different sorts. They may not be superhuman like the Incredibles but they're our gifts. Some of us are good writers, others good editors. Some of us are good singers, others good musicians. Some of us are good at sports, others good at dancing. Some of us are good at mathematics, others good at language arts. Indeed some of us seem to have many gifts and others of us have less, but all of us have gifts that are uniquely ours.

Our baptismal call requires us to discover our talents and gifts and then increase them by using them for the good of others. Sometimes this discovery is hard work. We often want other people's gifts, but that is envy. It will be ultimately destructive within us and towards them. Instead, we are called to discover our own gifts and direct them towards others. That is our work to discover and direct to others!

Imagine if we all took the time today to discover what we really love to do and what we are good at doing. Then we directed those gifts towards others. Whether it be singing or proclaiming here on Sundays, or speaking in front of people for your work during the week, or whether it be serving at the table here on Sundays, or serving the homeless in the shelters, or whether it be teaching in the classroom, or teaching your children at home, or whether visiting your family, or visiting the family-less. No matter what, our gifts can be turned towards the good of the entire family of humanity. I am totally convinced that if everyone present today were to genuinely discover their gifts, and then use them in service to others, we would be like the Incredibles acting together. And this family at Holy Spirit Parish would truly become an Incredible Christian Family.

Expressing Love Explicitly

In Newgrange, Ireland, there is an ancient Passage Tomb Monument built by a Neolithic community about 5,000 years ago. This pre-dates Stonehenge and even the Egyptian pyramids! On the entrance stone there are three circles intertwined as one image – a web spiral. This was, and is, a very important and sacred image for the Irish. Indeed, the circle has always been understood as a sacred image. As many of you know, the Celtic Cross has a circle behind the cross. In pre-Christian Ireland, the circle and the web spiral were important. So it is not surprising when St Patrick came to Ireland and tried to explain God as Trinity to the local people, he chose a shamrock leaf. He explained that the three leaves represented the three persons of God: Father, Son and Holy Spirit. The Celts immediately thought of their sacred image of three circles.

It was not difficult for the Celts to believe in St Patrick's message as their sacred symbol reflected his message. Indeed, it has been said that Ireland is one of the few countries in the world where no blood was shed when they were Christianised. Scholars maintain that St Patrick succeeded in his mission to Ireland because his message spoke to their experience of God. In other words, even though they were not able to express their belief, they believed in the mystery of the three-ness of God. They already participated in God even though they did not fully understand.

Today, the church celebrates the Most Holy Trinity. We celebrate not so much the 'doctrine' but the 'reality' of the Trinity. The reality of the Trinity is that God loves us. God expresses that love for us through the Son in the Holy Spirit. In the words of the gospel today, 'God so loved the world that he gave us his only Son, Christ Jesus.' Jesus then shows us how much the Father loves us by giving us the very gift the Father gave him – the Holy Spirit. God expresses his love for us explicitly through the actions of the persons of the Most Holy Trinity. The reality of the Trinity is all about God's explicit expression of love for us.

There are many things in life we find hard to express. One of these seems to be love itself. I am Irish and we are not known for expressing our affection! I mean when I left Ireland, immigrating here in 1989, I shook hands with my father at the airport and gave my mother a peck on the cheek as I said goodbye. This was the sum total of my expression of affection! That is how my culture taught me to express love. However, I think we are called to move beyond our cultural boundaries and no longer limit ourselves by our narrow understanding. God leads us by example in his explicit self-expression of love for us through the gift of his Son and his Holy Spirit.

To live the Trinity is to find a way to express our love for one another. There is no way that fits all people and so we need to find the expression that best fits our personality. One way I have learned since I arrived in the US is that of note-writing. A handwritten note saying, 'thank-you' or 'I love you' can be so powerful to our loved ones. It can be one way to express explicitly our love or gratitude to our parents, spouses, children, or even friends. Another way is through the doing of kind deeds for them. It does not matter what way we do it, the important thing is that we can find some way to explicitly express that love individually this week. Then, we will live the Trinity in our lives.

This week how can we explicitly express our love for one another both as individuals and as a community, thus living out the reality of the Trinity? The reality that God loves us explicitly.

Living Bread in the Hand

During World War II, the officers of the Third Reich's secret service forcefully recruited many 12 and 13-year-old boys into the Junior Gestapo. These harshly treated boys were given only inhumane jobs that they had to perform without rest or complaint.

After the war ended, most of these boys had lost contact with their families and wandered aimlessly, without food or shelter. As part of the aid programme to rebuild postwar Germany, many of these youth were housed in tent cities. There, doctors and nurses worked with them in an attempt to restore their mental, physical, and emotional health. It was an uphill battle.

Many of the boys would awaken several times during the night screaming in terror. One doctor had an idea for handling their fears. After serving the boys a hearty meal, he'd tuck them into bed with a piece of bread in their hands that they were told to save until morning. The boys began to sleep soundly after that because, after so many years of hunger and uncertainty as to their next meal, they finally had the assurance of food for the next day.[1]

This is precisely what God does for us. God gives us Jesus and Jesus gives us himself. In the celebration of the Eucharist each week, we recognise that Jesus gives his very self to us. He gives us not only bread to tuck away in our hands but he gives us his flesh to eat and blood to drink so that we can remain in him and he in us. He promises to be with us forever, no matter what happens in our lives. He gives us the assurance that we will not go hungry spiritually and that each day we will receive more food. We do not need to worry about our daily spiritual nourishment. Each week he offers us this living bread. Each week he promises to replenish our weary spirits. Each week he invites us to remain in him.

But there is more to this celebration of the Eucharist than just receiving. We are given a mission each and every week. We are called to go forth to share ourselves in the world we live in. We are called to bring that living bread into the world. St Augustine says it best. When we receive the Holy Communion, 'We be-

1. Patricia Datchuck Sanchez, 'Celebration: An Ecumenical Worship Resource,' (Kansas City, Missouri: National Catholic Reporter Company Inc, May, 2005)

come what we receive – the Body of Christ.' Yes, when we receive, we literally become the Body of Christ. We are then called to become that living bread to others and to become that blood poured out for others. We are called to receive here at this table and then we are compelled to share this living bread with others. We are invited to take some of our living bread and tuck it into the hands of someone in need or fear, so they can believe in God's promises. Our mission as disciples is to share what we have with others in need.

I do not want to make it sound so easy, because it is not. One of the things that often stops us from sharing more is the question about self-preservation. If I give this or that away, then what will I have for 'me'? If I share my time, then where is the time for myself? If I share my gifts with others, then when do I reap my own benefits? If I share my treasures, then what about my personal wants? You see the Lord promises to replenish whatever we share, whether it be time, talent, or treasure. If we share and return to this table, he *will* replenish us and we will have enough.

Let me give you an example. Last summer I was hiking with a friend of mine in Canyonlands, Utah. This particular day, it was going to be very hot. So we set off very early in order to finish hiking before the heat of the day. Even though we started hiking at 6am and hiked well, at 9am it was already 110 degrees and we were already running out of water. Actually, I had gone through three quarters of my water already but my friend had only gone through one third of his water. We stopped and accessed the situation, realising that we were definitely in trouble as we still had to hike out of the hot canyon. We took what water we had, divided it equally and rationed ourselves for the rest of the long hike out of the canyon. Without my friend's willingness to share what little he had, we would not have made it out of that canyon of 110 degrees. Together we shared, together we hiked out.

We are called to look at our lives in much the same way and share what little we have, whether that be time, talent, or treasure. As we celebrate this Feast Day of the Most Holy Body and Blood of Christ may we truly recognise that we become what we receive. We become that living bread for others. We become that blood poured out for others. This week may we find someone in need and tuck the living bread into their hands.

Christt the Candle

'I will make you a light to the nations, that my salvation will reach to the ends of the earth.' The function of a candle is to give light to others. No matter the size of the candle, its function is the same – giving light. How does it do this? It burns itself to give light. It cannot give light without giving of itself.[1] In other words, it gives its very self so others will have light. The gospels use this exact analogy for Christ and discipleship.

At the beginning of the gospel of John, we hear that Jesus is the light of the human race 'and his light shines in the darkness and the darkness has not overcome it. A man named John was sent from God. He came for testimony, to testify to the light so that all might believe through him. He was not the light but came to testify to the light' (John 1:5-8). In today's gospel, we hear John do exactly that, testifying to Jesus as the light of the world. It was for this reason that John preached. Yes, Jesus is the light of the world and we are called to be likewise. We are called to be like the candle, giving of our very selves for the life of others.

A great example of giving life to others is the relationship we have with our children. Good parents give of their very lives for the sake of their children. They spend themselves for the sake of their children. They consume their precious time and give it to their children. They would give everything for their children. Just last week, this reality became even clearer for me as I had the pleasure of visiting with my brother and sister-in-law to welcome their new baby boy, Sean Paul. To see this newborn baby in his mother's arms and recognise that she gave of her very self in giving birth to him. Yes, only days ago, Maria had Sean in her womb giving life to him. And even now, he depends completely on her for his nourishment. For the rest of his life, he will look to his parents for life in one form or another. Yes, the pre-eminent example of the Christian disciple is the good parent who takes care of their children and supplies their every need for the goodness of the child. Parents, know that you do the work of the Lord when you are a good parent. Know that you are a Christian dis-

1. Patricia Datchuck Sanchez, 'Celebration: An Ecumenical Worship Resource,' (Kansas City, Montana: National Catholic Reporter Company, Inc, January 2005).

ciple when you spend yourself for the sake of your children. Know that you are walking the light of the Lord and shining his light on the path of your children's lives.

For the rest of us who do not have children, we are called to spend ourselves for the sake of others. Not to spend our time and gifts on just ourselves, but to consume ourselves and give life to others. We are called to shine our light brightly for all to see that the true light of the world is Christ. We are called to move beyond the 'self' and live for the 'other'. We are called to be like the candle and consume ourselves so that others can have life.

This week, may we know that when we are good parents and give of our time, talents, and treasure to our children, we are consuming ourselves for their sakes; we are spending our light so that they can have light. May we know that when we live for others, giving selflessly to their needs, we are burning our light for others to see. This week, may we consume ourselves as a candle does, so that others may see that Christ is truly the light of the world.

Passing on the Baton

During the summer, we had the opportunity to watch some of the greatest athletes in the world compete. I am not sure which event was your favorite but for me the most memorable event was the relay race. Usually, the strongest runner takes the last leg of the race so he or she can make up for what the others lacked. That position is called the anchor position. However, the critical time in every relay race is the passing and receiving of the baton. The fastest runners in the world will not win a relay race if they cannot pass the baton. Many a race has been lost on the failure of the baton passing.

Well, in today's gospel, we hear how John the Baptist passes the baton of the message of God to Jesus. Indeed, Jesus is the anchor who will make up for whatever all the other prophets have lacked over history. You see over the history of humanity, from Abraham to John the Baptist, prophets have been sent from God to deliver the message of God. That message was simply to remain faithful to God and to turn away from sin. Today, we hear how the last of the Old Testament prophets, John the Baptist, hands this baton to Christ, who in turn will run the last leg of the race. Indeed, Jesus does make up for every prophet and all humanity, winning the race, and assuring us eternal life.

But Jesus calls others to help spread that message of eternal life. He enlists some new disciples and gives each of them a baton. This baton is the message of God: the command to love God and to love one another. This same baton is given to all the disciples, not just to Peter and Paul. These disciples then pass the baton, the good news, to all who were willing to listen. This same baton is passed on to us by our parents, and by their parents before them. Now it comes to us, and we are called to pass the baton to others. It is the critical time in the race of our lives, passing on the faith. It is critical that we get this right as we pass on the faith to our children, our friends, and our neighbours. We do this by living the message first, then by loving one another. We do it by being the message. Then our children, our friends, and our neighbours will get the message very clearly. We do this as a community when we pass on the faith to the candidates and catechumens of the RCIA process, to the children who are in preparation for receiving their first communion, and to the children who are being baptised this weekend. Each in our own way is passing on the faith, passing the baton to those who seek the good news. It is not just the families who pass on this faith. All of us present say we will live the faith as we pass it on.

Today, we continue to celebrate Christian Unity Week. The Pope has asked us to remember that all Christians, no matter what denomination, are baptised into the one Lord and one Christ. We are called to remember that they are our brothers and sisters in the faith. We are called to emphasise what we have in common and not on where we disagree or where we have conflict. In today's second reading, Paul writes to the Corinthians, admonishing them for causing division in the Body of Christ. He tells them that they have missed the point: there is no 'I'm for Paul,' or 'I'm for Apollos,' or 'I'm for Peter.' There is only Christ. Christ was crucified for all of us. We are all baptised into that one Christ. It is through him that we share in eternal life. Everyone who has been baptised into Christianity, no matter what denomination or church; no matter if Episcopalian, Methodist, Lutheran, or Presbyterian; no matter if in Africa, in Asia, in Europe, or right next door, everyone baptised into Christianity is baptised into the same Christ and is a member of that Body of Christ and part of the People of God.

So especially in this week of Christian Unity, may we recognise the unity of our baptismal promises. May we recognise that we all have been given this baton of faith and that there is two-thirds of the world's population that have yet to hear that message of Christianity. We can emphasise our unity and live the message of God, loving one another and loving God, and pass on the baton of faith to those who have not yet heard the message of God.

Habits of the Heart

Dental hygienists tell us that if we want clean and healthy teeth, we ought to brush our teeth for two full minutes using at least four different motions of the toothbrush. How many of us do that? To top it off, they tell us that we need to do so after every meal. Here's another health tip. In order to keep our hands thoroughly clean from bacteria, we ought to wash our hands using warm flowing water with plenty of soap for at least thirty seconds many times a day. How many of us do that? Imagine our children actually washing their hands for thirty seconds every time they got dirty. We are generally happy if they wash them at all.[1]

Both health tips are indeed true. But most of us say something like, 'Yeah right ... like, who really does that?' Sure, we acknowledge that it is the right thing to do but it seems so impractical and impossible for us to do it every time. Most of us are happy if we brush our teeth once a day for a minute and floss our teeth once a year, and wash our hands whenever we can get a chance.

Well, I think that is the same thing that happens with today's gospel. We hear one of the most popular readings from the gospel. It is from the Sermon on the Mount and today's passage is called the 'Beatitudes'. Yes, we acknowledge that these are good and virtuous things to be, but they are really not for us. They seem too impractical or impossible for us. 'Who really does that?' we ask ourselves. We shrug them off as some unattainable goal. Yet, just like the hygienists' advice about brushing teeth and cleaning hands, we know that these are true to life. We acknowledge them as truths to be lived, but cannot seem to get our heads or our lives around them. So where are we to go?

We saw today that there are some of us who do manage to actually do all the things that the hygienists tell us. What are the differences between them and the rest of us? How is it that some of us manage to do them and others don't? I think it is discipline. First, we need to make a decision to always do it. And then we

---

1. Adapted from Jim Auer, 'Celebration: An Ecumenical Worship Resource,' (Kansas City, Montana: National Catholic Reporter Company, Inc, January 2005).

go about practising that discipline until it becomes an embedded habit of life.

Let me give you an example. I was visiting my niece and nephew a couple of weeks ago. Each of them, ages 5 and 7, brush their teeth for two minutes, using one of those little children's electronic toothbrushes. They brush just before bed and first thing in the morning. Their teeth are not so dirty that they actually need that cleaning. But, it is a discipline that my brother and his wife are instilling in them. No matter where they travel, the children continue the discipline of brushing their teeth daily. It is one of those very good habits that, when they grow up, they will not even think about doing. Another example is that of washing hands. Because I meet and shake so many people's hands, I feel it is good for both me, and for the people whose hands I shake, to wash my hands frequently. So before and after every Mass, I wash my hands as prescribed. Actually, I wash my hands probably twenty to thirty times a day. And I rarely get a cold or the flu. It is all about discipline. Once it is instilled in us, we operate almost automatically.

The same can be said of living the gospel values. As disciples of Christ, we are called to work on this discipline. The discipline suggested in today's gospel is that of the beatitudes. If we look at these values, we actually do practise them in some ways. And we are called to practise them even more. For example, did you have someone hurt you, and you decided to forgive them, saying, 'Don't worry about it. Let's forget it'? Blessed are the merciful. Or have you been in a situation when you knew the right thing to do but you struggled with doing it, tempted to just not do so? Blessed are those who hunger and thirst for righteousness. Or have you been with someone who you knew was wrong in what he or she said? Knowing the truth, you decided not to correct them. You chose to not crush their spirit and you remained silent. Blessed are the meek and humble. And the list goes on.

I do not want to go through the whole list for you here. We need to look at the Bible and really reflect on these words. We are being called to develop good disciplines and habits. To do so, we really need to decide on how we act. Today, and this week, may we open up our Bible and look again at Matthew 5:1-12, and discern ways to develop new habits of the heart.

A Pinch of Salt in the World

As we continue to hear from the Sermon on the Mount in today's gospel, we continue to be challenged in the ways of discipleship. This whole sermon is instruction on what it means to be a disciple. Last week we heard the beatitudes and how we are called to specifically act in this world, while accepting that our reward may not come till the next world. We were called to act with discipline, developing good habits of the heart. Today, Jesus uses two metaphors to help illustrate this discipleship. He tells his disciples that they are the salt of the earth and the light of the world. Let's explore these for a minute.

The essence of salt is in its action. By itself, salt has no purpose. It exists for the good of the whole. Only when it is mixed with other things is salt's value brought to life. For example, a pinch of salt added to any kind of food, from meat and fish to popcorn and candy, brings out the natural flavour. It allows the fullness of something else to come to life. It is also a purifying and preserving agent. Again, it cannot purify or preserve anything on its own. It must be added to something before its value comes out.

When we examine light we find its essence is also in its action. Light on its own has no value or use. For example, if we took a flashlight and put it in a box sealed tight, what purpose does it have? None! Or, as Jesus puts it today in the gospel, we do not put a lamp in a bushel basket. No, the value of light is apparent only when it comes in contact with something. Light transforms the cold of night into the warm, safety of day. Light gives life to plants and animals. Sometimes, it is hard for us to fully appreciate the significance of sunlight. But, just for a moment, imagine what life would be like without artificial light. Imagine if we had to rely completely on sunlight. We would be amazed how our days would be different as we depend on light for so much. All activities of the evening would come to an end. All plants and animals rely on sunlight for their very existence, their warmth, and the required nourishment to grow. Yes, when light shines, it gives life to whatever it shines upon. The value of light comes alive in its action.

Just as the value of salt and light is in their actions, so too, the value of our discipleship is in our actions. The essence of our discipleship is in what we do. We are called to add value to the lives of others in the way we act in our daily life. Like salt, we are called to bring out the natural goodness in others. Like light, we are called to illuminate the good in others. Maybe instead of criticising the weakness in others, we can point to their strengths. Instead of putting down someone in word or action, we can find the gift that they are to the world. It is so easy to focus on the weaknesses of others and much harder to notice their strengths. We can be one who believes in others and shine the light in their darkness. We can be the one who helps others discover their gifts and enable them to use these gifts for the good of others. We can be the one who always brings out the natural goodness in others. But we need to decide to be that sort of person. You would be surprised how easy it is to transform a person's life. Even a genuine smile can transform a person's dreary day. Maybe we laugh at some of their jokes, even if they are not funny. Yes, we can transform the lives of others by what we say and do. So today, may we bring our discipleship into action by being salt in the world, adding to the goodness of others, or by being light to those in darkness. Today, if we can be just a pinch of salt or a ray of light.

Sometimes is Now

I recently had the opportunity to see the Broadway musical *Brooklyn*. It is the story of a young girl named Brooklyn, who was born out of wedlock in Paris, France and ends up being a great actress. However, her heart yearns to meet her real father. So, she sets off to find him in Brooklyn, New York. Eventually, she encounters him and invites him into her life.

Taylor, young Brooklyn's father, is now presented with a choice: to leave his old, familiar way of life in the shadows of the streets of Brooklyn or come into the light and embrace this new life set before him with a child he never knew he had.

There's a beautiful song he sings called 'Sometimes' in which he outlines his struggle to choose: 'The world is a stage and we are the players,' he says. 'Sometimes a villain, sometimes a saviour. Do we choose the roles? Do we write our own lines? A lifetime of asking and I'm left with "Sometimes".' The song goes on to say that the 'sometimes' is now. It is a great musical about life and how we can choose to live it. This is not some fickle choice like whether I would like milk or cream in my coffee but rather a choice that determines his way of life.

Yes, we always have choices to make in our lives. Sometimes our choices are limited. Sometimes, we feel forced into choices we'd rather not make. Sometimes, it is easy, and sometimes it is not. Sometimes, they are small and fickle; other times, they are major and life changing. But the way of life we choose is always for us to decide. At any point along the way, we can choose to be different. Being a Christian is the choice of a way of life.

Life choices are the theme of today's scripture. The first reading from the Book of Sirach outlines the choice that lies before all people in all of time: to keep God's commandments and follow the Lord God; to choose life and goodness over death and evil. In the gospel, we hear the continuation of the Sermon on the Mount where Jesus is reminding them of their obligation to the law.

Today, we have before us a choice, too. We are called to choose to follow Christ in every way. We are called to leave behind our former way of life. This is huge decision that will inform our whole life.

We are all here each Sunday and so we can say we already believe. However, sometimes, the sharpness of our Christianity is dulled and we just plod along not really challenging ourselves as Christians. Sometimes, we need to renew our way of life as a Christian. Sometimes, we need to realise the radical way of life that we have been called to live as Christians. The 'sometime' is now!

Our choice to believe in Christ must inform our every decision. It is not a fickle choice but a life choice. We always look for the way to follow Christ. We always look for the way to love others; to forgive and be reconciled with others, and so to serve others.

Yes, we are called to serve and love others. For each of us, this loving enterprise will be different. For some of us, this will mean forgiving some old or new grudge; it's going to be hard to let go of that hurt. For others of us, it will mean being nice to someone at school or the office who we really do not like nor enjoy their company; it's going to be hard to pleasant and kind to them. For some others of us, it will be to stretch out to those in need maybe in our very own families; it will be hard to submit to, and serve their neediness.

For all of us, the choices will be hard and not straight forward; it will not be coffee with milk or coffee with cream. It will be a radical choice to follow Christ. We come out of the shadows of the streets of our lives and step into the light of Christ: To be known as a Christian, to live as a Christian, to stand and make the choice of choosing Christ. The 'sometime' is now. We choose Christ.

Unpack Your Bags

Before I became a priest, my work as an executive took me travelling around the world, clocking more than 100,000 miles a year by airplane. Sometimes I would find myself in three different countries within the same week. To make the most of that much travelling, I had a habit whenever I got to a hotel: I completely unpacked all my clothes, putting them into the drawers or closet and totally emptying my suitcases. It was my way of moving in and making it home! Whether I would be there for 1 day or 10 days, I unpacked everything and made that place my home for the time I would stay. I was totally committed to that location. If I did not unpack, I always felt I was living temporarily and was ready to leave at any time. It was my way of staying sane in a crazy travel schedule.

This can be a great metaphor for relationships, especially married couples. When a couple gets married and moves into a house together, they have to do the same thing. I mean, if one person does not unpack everything and keeps some boxes ready in case things do not work out, we would think it a bit strange to say the least! We would wonder if they are really committed to the marriage. There would be little chance that the marriage would last long, as one person is really not committed and is always waiting for the escape route.

During the week, I caught a part of a dialogue on television between two characters explaining the dynamics of marriage. I think it speaks well to this matter of commitment. He said that a 'commitment is not a real commitment unless it has no expiration date.' I think that's a wonderful way to explain marriage. There is no expiration date. That's what makes it so challenging and yet so awesome. A married couple signs up in total commitment to their spouse for their entire life without knowing what's ahead. That's what makes it so awesome, indeed.

Christian marriage is considered to be the exemplar, the best example, of Christian discipleship. We look to married couples to witness their love for one another and to witness their love for their children. In doing so, we witness an authentic love at work. I'm not saying that every marriage is paragon of virtue but I am saying that two people living in marriage aspire to that ideal. And when it works, it works beautifully. That sort of love is hard work by any standard and many of you can attest to this fact.

Today's gospel gives us lots of examples of what this Christian love looks like in action. This authentic love for another is more than just doing good by our spouses, children, parents or friends who will repay us back in some way. 'Do not tax collectors do the same?' (Matt 5:46) Instead, we are called to treat everyone as family or close friends. In today's gospel, Jesus continues his great Sermon on the Mount telling his disciples, and us, if they love their enemies and do good for them then their reward will be great. This is not *quid quo pro*, it is Christian discipleship.

We are called to be totally committed to being disciples. It is a total commitment and not a temporary one. There is no expiration date on our baptism or our baptismal promises which we renew every week. Yes, we are called to love others.

We are called to live out this commandment today. We are called to love our enemies. We may not think we have enemies but there are many who consider us their enemies. In faraway lands of Iraq, Afghanistan or other such countries, they despise everything we are as Americans and they really hate us for who we are. That may be because of ignorance or fear by some people. Or maybe it's because of deliberate misguidance on behalf of a few hardened leaders, eager to take as much power as they can receive. Either way, there are many who consider us enemies. How we treat them in action will proclaim louder than our words what our beliefs are as a nation.

Yet, that is not really where we have the most influence. We have the most influence in our homes, schools, and offices. Yes, we can fight for peace throughout the world and that's a good thing indeed. But our real fight for peace is in our daily lives. We are called to stretch out to those in our community whom are disadvantaged or whom we dislike, maybe even hate.

We are called to put down our weapons of violence whether they are violent actions or violent words. We are called to unpack all our belongings and be in for the long-term relationship of being a disciple. We are called to love and not seek revenge. We are called to love and not seek repayment. We are called to love and not harbour ill will. We are called to love and serve others. Our discipleship is not a temporary stay but a stay without an expiration date. So, let's unpack our bags for the Christian life and be ready for total commitment this week.

Deepen Our Roots

The *Moso* is a bamboo plant that grows in China and the Far East. After the Moso is planted, no visible growth occurs for up to 5 years – not even under ideal conditions! It appears to just sit there without any growth. Then, as if by magic, it suddenly begins to grow at the rate of nearly two and one half feet per day, reaching a full height of ninety feet within just six weeks. Of course, it is not magic at all. The Moso's rapid growth is due to the miles of roots it develops during those first five years. Then it can withstand the tough seasonal weather typical of the Far East.[1]

In today's first reading, the prophet Isaiah warns the people of the day, and us, that we ought to rely on God alone. We ought not put our trust in humans but solely in God. We ought to put our roots deep down in the God's soil, so we have a good foundation for the weather of our lives. If we do so, the Lord tells us that we will bear great fruit. We will be able to withstand the storms of our lives. We will be like a tree planted alongside a river, never worrying about water or nourishment. We are called to put our trust in God alone.

In today's gospel, Jesus cautions his disciples, and us, about caring for earthly possessions. 'No one can serve two masters. He will either love one and hate the other, or be devoted to one and despise the other. You cannot serve God and mammon' (Mt 6:24-25). Jesus reverses the common wisdom of the time that said those who had wealth were considered to blessed. Instead, Jesus says those who trust in the Lord are blessed. He tells us that those who rely on God will be rewarded. He warns us to not depend on material possessions but instead depend on God in all matters. Not to worry about the future as he will care for us.

The story of the Moso bamboo can help us. The plant sinks its roots deep into the soil and searches hard for the nutrients it requires for growth. When the root system is prepared, it then grows. As Christians, we are called to put our roots deep into God's Word, so we can find the nutrients that we need for our

---

1. Brian Cavanaugh, 'The Sower's Seeds,' (Mahwah, New Jersey: Paulist Press, 1990) #45.

spiritual growth. Often, there seems to be very little visible growth but we all know, if we take the journey seriously, there is a lot of interior preparation work happening. We are preparing our root system.

We are called to put our roots deep into the soil of God. It is there that we will receive the necessary nutrients for our required spiritual growth. It is there that we will receive the strength to endure all things. It is there that we will become a disciple of Christ. Then, like the bamboo, we will be able to sway and bend with the troubles of our life without breaking. Then we will be firmly planted in the Lord's soil. How do we develop our roots?

In order to know the will of God, we need to spend some time with him. We start that process here in this celebration of the Eucharist each Sunday but it is not enough for it to end here. To really understand and know the Lord's plan for us, we need to commit to spend some time with him. And that means spending time in prayer. If our prayer wanes, so too does our enthusiasm for the Lord.

From my own personal experience, let me assure you that if we pray, our lives become different; we realise energy we did not know we had. If we commit to just a few minutes of prayer every day, the Lord will fill us and we will be genuinely blessed by God. This week, may we deepen our roots for spiritual growth and be like the bamboo in bad weather – able to sway and bend but not break! May we deepen our roots in God's soil.

Two Sides of the Same Coin

Many years ago, I had the opportunity to travel to Jerusalem on a pilgrimage to the Holy Land. I was travelling on Israeli Airlines and there were a lot of Orthodox Jews travelling on the same airplane. At one point on this long flight from San Francisco to Jerusalem, the Orthodox Jews rose to their feet and moved into the aisles. They tied plastic black boxes to their wrists with plastic string, and tied a little black box to their forehead and around their head. Then they started to pray, singing psalms as they swayed.

They were doing exactly what today's first reading from Deuteronomy said to do. Inside those small boxes are scrolls with this prayer: 'Hear, O Israel! The LORD is our God, the LORD alone! Therefore, you shall love the LORD, your God, with all your heart, and with all your soul, and with all your strength. Take to heart these words which I enjoin on you today' (Deut 6:5-6). Moses encouraged them to always keep these words on their minds that they may always direct the work of their hands. The Orthodox Jews still pray these words several times a day. They put the words close to their minds and literally on their wrists to direct their work of their hands. They also place similar little metal boxes with scrolls over every doorpost in their houses.

These words are very important to the Jews and Christians alike. Jesus makes them interdependent and linked to one another. He makes the two into one commandment; two sides to the same coin. Jesus says to make our prayers with God come into reality with our neighbour, this is what we must do. We cannot love God without loving our neighbour. And when we love our neighbour, we love God. We cannot have a coin with just heads or a coin with just tails. A coin always has two sides, heads and tails; love God and love your neighbours.

In the same way Jesus challenges the Jews of his time not to just pray those words by tying them to their bodies, we are challenged not just to come here on Sundays for prayer, but to live that prayer by loving our neighbour. This is a real challenge for all of us. This means the one person in our school, office, or neighbourhood that really irks us, is the person we have to love.

It seems easy enough to love our family and friends, although we know that has its challenges, too! But it becomes harder when we are called to love that person who is homeless or destitute and needy. Even if they are there because of bad choices in their life, we are called to love them. Yes, that is exactly what we are called to do.

It gets even harder when we are called to love someone who hates us. Our neighbour is everyone. We cannot insulate ourselves and pretend that we are to love only those who love us; our family and friends or those who are nice to us. Jesus tells us: 'for even the thieves and robbers love their friends.' We are called, as Christians, to love God with our all heart, mind, soul, and strength *and* to love all of our neighbours in the same way.

I am not saying it is easy; it's not easy at all. But that is our work as disciples in Christ. We are called to find a way to reach out to that one person in the class, in the office, or in the neighbourhood and find a way to love and forgive them despite their actions. Or to reach out to that homeless person or that person who has nobody else; to find a way to reach out and serve their need. That's what we are called to do as a result of the Sunday liturgy.

This week, we are all challenged to love in different ways. But we all have to find a way to love others. We must take what we celebrate at this table and put it into action in our daily lives. That's Christ's challenge to us today; two sides to the same coin of love: one side to love God; the other side to love our neighbours. There is no other currency in Christianity but love.

Today as we leave, we are challenged to not stop here at this table, as if to tie a prayer box to head or arms for this hour; we are challenged to take it with us in our lives. When a person really irritates us, we can immediately go into action and begin to forgive and love that person. Maybe, when we see someone in need, we can step up to help. Or we can actively seek out those in need and serve them. Or maybe, we can pray for reconciliation for our world in this time of distress.

No matter what the challenge is for us personally, the currency of Christianity is love. Two sides to that coin: love God and love our neighbour. We must to do both.

I Am a Sinner

'My name is John and I am an alcoholic.'[1] These or similar words, typically, start every Alcoholics Anonymous (AA) meeting. It is the first step in the twelve-step programme of recovery. Anyone who attends an AA meeting recognises the need for anonymity even as they publicly admit their addiction and weakness; it is the start of the path to healing. However, the absolute first step in that process of recovery of one's life is to acknowledge that they have a problem. One cannot address a solution until one accepts that one has a problem. But the purpose of the first step is to immediately move to the second step where they acknowledge that God has the power to heal and restore them. Those steps sound so easy but they can be so hard. To admit publicly, and authentically, that one has a problem is not easy at all and then to admit that only God can bring us healing and life. Yes, it is simple but not easy at all. I think we, as Christians, can learn a lot from our recovering brothers and sisters. Their spirituality is a worthwhile example of Christian discipleship.

In today's gospel, Jesus tells us that he came to save, not the righteous, but sinners. Our first step as Christians is to admit that we are indeed sinners in need of God's mercy. It is God who does the saving and we have to co-operate with God. Of course, we cannot do this in an unauthentic way, and just say, 'I'm a sinner' and then continue sinning. We really need to ponder what we do and how it hurt others. Our sins are not just what we 'do' but also what we 'fail to do'. We need to consider that what we fail to do hurts others, too. We are called to notice people who are in desperate need, whom we do not even notice whether they are homeless, jobless, or friendless, and tend to their needs in some way. Yes, we are all sinners in need of God's mercy and we need to start with that sentence, 'Hi, my name is Brendan and I am a sinner.'

But just like AA, the purpose of the first step is to accept the challenge in our life and then to move beyond it by accepting the solution. When we take the first step, we are called to quickly

---

1. Inspired by use in Patricia Datchuck Sanchez, 'Celebration: An Ecumenical Worship Resource,' (Kansas City, Montana: National Catholic Reporter Company, Inc, June 2005).

take the second step and admit that God has the power to heal and restore us. Oh yes, that sounds simple but it, too, is not easy. God has the power to overcome any hurdle. Today's second reading from St Paul to the Romans illustrates that power. Paul highlights the faith of Abraham, who believed that God would fulfill God's promise of giving Abraham many children. Yes, God can work wonders in our lives as he did for Abraham if only we allow him to do so. So, the second step is to acknowledge that God has the power to changes all things, and allow God to touch us with his steadfast love and his enduring mercy.

In the history of the church there have been times when we emphasised the importance of the first step and focused on our sinfulness to an extreme. We were reminded often about our sinfulness and unworthiness, sometimes through fiery sermons, to the point we may have felt hopeless and despondent. Then there are other times in our church when the importance of God's mercy and forgiveness were emphasised to an extreme. We were reminded of how God loves us no matter what. There is nothing we can do to fend off this loveable, old man in the sky, sometimes forgetting to acknowledge that we have sinned at all. When in fact, it is necessary to take both steps and embrace both extremes. We do not want to take the first step without the second nor the second without the first. We need to first acknowledge our sin and then embrace God's grace to save us. It sounds so easy but it is quite hard to do.

Today and this week, may we take the challenge of the gospel to follow the Lord by first authentically acknowledging our sins. Then allow God's mercy to fill us and heal us, bringing us to 'new life in Christ Jesus'. Today, may we take that first step and acknowledge, if only in the private of our own room, 'Hi, my name is Brendan, and I am a sinner.'

11th Sunday in Ordinary Time
Exodus 19:2-6; Psalm 100; Romans 5:6-11; Matthew 9:36-10:8

Without Cost You Have Received

Without cost you have received. Without cost you are to give.
(Matthew 10:8)

My dad had a favourite story with which he illustrated his understanding of faith and the need to be generous. 'Once there was young boy who visited his elderly grandfather. That particular day, his grandfather was planting a small apple tree in his garden. He asked, "Grandpa, when will that tree give apples?" The grandfather answered gently, "This is a very small seedling and it will take many years before it can produce fruit for others. And your grandpa will be long gone before then." "Then why bother planting it if you will not eat its apples?" he challenged. "My dear child, for many years I have eaten from trees in this garden and I never planted any of them. My father and grandfather planted them. So today, I plant this tree for you so that you and your friends will have apples to eat".'

Yes, without cost we have received and without cost we are to give. Most of the things in this life we have received as total gifts: our health, our families, our world, our very selves. We are called to give, to share with others our health, our families, our world, our very selves. As Christians, we believe that is the circle of life of our world. We pass through here for a short time and we are called to share what we have with others, most especially our faith in God.

And what is the motivation? It comes from the realisation that everything we are is gift from God. Indeed, the greatest gift that God offers, through Christ, is the gift of eternal life. This is what we celebrate every Sunday when we come around this table. We celebrate that Christ offered himself while we were still sinners, so that we could have eternal life and the knowledge of eternal life. We then celebrate with great joy what God offers us and live with the knowledge of eternal life. Now that ought to change our lives in some real ways. Today, God, through the scriptures, challenges us again to share our gifts with others. And when we share, we are challenged not to become discouraged if we do not see results.

Yes, we pass on our faith to our children and sometimes do not see the fruit of our labour. We wonder where all the values that we instilled in our children have gone. We wonder why they don't go to church anymore. We wonder if we will ever see the fruit of our labour. Well, that is true for a lot of things we do in this life.

For example, this week marks the end of the school year for most schoolchildren and their teachers. It is a bittersweet experience for the teachers. On one hand, they are delighted to have vacation for the summer. But on the other hand, they will not see these children again. They have spent a whole year teaching them so many things and now they are gone. They will not see the fruit of their labour. But each year these teachers go back to their jobs with the same enthusiasm and energy as the first year. They will continue to impart all the knowledge they can, knowing, with faith, that their efforts will bear fruit, albeit unseen for now.

The twelve apostles selected by Jesus were sent with a mission to go and proclaim the good news of Christ. They would not have seen much of the fruit of their labour. Yet, they were not discouraged by the 'lack of results' and gave the same enthusiasm and energy as the first days of their ministry. We too, are called to work in the vineyard of the Lord. We, too, are called to go and proclaim the good news of Christ, sharing the knowledge we have, the faith we have, sharing our time, talents, and treasures with others. We, too, must plant, knowing that we might not see the fruit of our labours. We, too, are called to give with the same enthusiasm and energy each day. Today, may we find one new way to share with others. Today, may we not become discouraged in the sharing that we do. Today, without cost we have received. Today, without cost we are to give.

12th Sunday in Ordinary Time
Jeremiah 20:10-13; Psalm 69; Romans 5:12-15; Matthew 10:26-33

Fear Factor: Christian Edition

Recently, I had the opportunity to watch a television show called 'Fear Factor: Couples Edition.' There are actually many editions of 'Fear Factor' such as 'Miss America Edition', 'Friends Edition', and 'Family Edition' to name but a few of these reality shows. I found this TV programme fascinating. For those of you who have never seen it, the show is about people doing all sorts of weird things. Sometimes they walk about the outside ledge of the top story of a skyscraper, or they pick up flags from a rotating device 100 feet above water. Sometimes, they do something under water, or they eat strange things. Why would people do such things? What is the incentive to attempt to push oneself to the limit? The answer is easy – money, a chance at $50,000. One has to ask, how did they think of such things to do? Many may already know, but it is part of the interview process. Any future participants have to declare their fears and these fears are then confirmed by their close friends. In other words, these strange and bizarre stunts are supplied by the imagination of the participants themselves. So they have the incentive and the fear, but they still must go through their fears to the other side.

In today's gospel, Jesus tells us not to be afraid of anyone or anything. In one sense, he is calling us to play, in real life 'Fear Factor: Christian Edition.' We need to ask ourselves, what is our incentive? Why would we go to so much trouble during life? Sometimes we think the incentive is eternal life or salvation but that is already promised to us by our baptism. As Christ came to save everyone, we only need to accept that offer. Instead, our incentive is not only eternal life and our promise of eternal bliss, but living the fullness of that reality here and now. Our incentive is to be able to live life to the fullest right now. To become more fully who we were made to be. If I am John, with certain gifts, then I am called to be fully John and use those gifts for others. If I am Mary, with different gifts, then I am called to be more fully Mary and use those gifts for others. That is living life to the fullest, living life for others and knowing that we can give them joy in our sharing. It is not some self-indulgent joy, but a joy of being selfless. Yes, our incentive is to be more fully who we were created to be, and to allow God's grace to flow through us. No matter what our joys or sorrows, our sadness or happiness, we know that we have eternal life through Christ and we celebrate that reality here every Sunday.

So, we have the incentive, and now we need to face our fears. Like the participants for the 'Fear Factor' show, we who want to play the 'Christian Edition' need to sit down and list our fears with complete honesty. If we are truthful with ourselves then we will acknowledge that we all have some fears that disable us from being more fully alive. We have fears that cover us with a frost that makes us immobile and freezes our movement and development in our spiritual lives.

Some of us are deadly afraid of public speaking; not just speaking in front of large crowds, but in front of any crowds greater than one. This leaves us incapable of offering any opinion or insight on anything. No, instead, God is offering us his grace to break through that frozen reality and let the light of Christ shine in our darkness. God is calling us to break through our fears into freedom.

Some of us are deadly afraid of conflict and avoid any and all confrontation, even when things are dysfunctional. We ignore the desperate need to face certain abuses in our household or office to avoid confrontation. In doing so, we enable the dysfunction to continue. Instead, God is calling us to break through that darkness into his wonderful light.

Some of us are deadly afraid of intimacy and avoid any new friends for fear of being hurt. We take no risks and therefore have no new friends or opportunities for growth or new life. Instead, God is calling us to proclaim from the housetops, our new life, and invite others to that path of Christ. God is calling all of us to new life in him.

Today, may we take seriously this 'Fear Factor: Christian Edition' and be honest enough with ourselves to list our fears; to allow God's grace to shine through the darkness of our fears and pass through our fears into freedom. Our incentive is to live life fully here and now. This week, may we be free from fear and free to live.

Stand Up, Let Go, and Be Free For Christ

Psychologists tell us there are three different types of relationships: healthy relationships, dependent and/or dysfunctional relationships, and mutually dependent and/or dysfunctional relationships. I am talking here about the normative person's relationships, not about the different pathologies and psychoses that exist. Fortunately, most of us do not deal with these. These different relationships are best illustrated through a simple demonstration which I learned many years ago.

I need some volunteers for this part. Thank you, John and Mary. I ask you to stand facing each other and raise your hands with your palms facing each other as if to lean on each other. Imagine that we relate through our hands. If we touch our palms together then we are in relationship. When all of us are standing upright, we can easily engage and disengage without much effort; we can touch palms without effort. If one of us decides to let go without informing the other, no real damage is done. We just stop 'relating' for that moment. We can even relate to a number of people at once. These are called healthy relationships. We can engage and disengage without hurting one another.

Now touch palms again. This time I ask Mary to lean on John and move your feet back away from him. Now you are leaning on him completely and John can feel the pressure of your whole body through his hands. If either of you let go, Mary, you will fall and hurt yourself, but John will remain standing, unharmed. Only Mary can be hurt in this scenario. Now, Mary, stand up.

This time I ask John to move his feet back leaning on Mary. In this scenario Mary can feel the pressure of John. Because John is a heavier person, we can tell by Mary's red face that this is hard work for her. If either of you let go, John will be the only one who will fall and get hurt. Mary will remain standing unscathed by the incident. These two are called dependent relationships and can often be dysfunctional in adults. One person is always under pressure and feels that strain. If one lets go the other will be hurt immediately.

Now I ask both of you to lean on each other. In this scenario, both of you can reach an equilibrium point where you are leaning on each other and it feels quite comfortable. However, if either of you let go, both will fall and be harmed. This relationship can feel quite good at first, but after awhile, we grow tired. This is called a mutually dependent relationship and is nearly always dysfunctional and detrimental for both people.

When we are children, our relationship with our parents is one of complete dependence. That is a natural stage we go through but it is a passing phase which we outgrow. We soon learn to stand up and let go of our parents. Sometimes we, parents, can become dependent on them to equalise their dependency on us. When children grow up and let go, as often happens in the teenage years, they assert their independence. We get hurt as we fall in response to their new independence. Rather, we are called to have an independent relationship in which we engage and disengage without pain or discomfort. The healthy relationship is one of independence.

There are other relationships in which we can feel the dependence of others and it feels good. We remain in control and needed. If we let go, the other person falls and we instinctively know it. It feels good to be needed and depended upon. This is fine for a short time but is unhealthy for any long period.

Then there are other relationships in which we are as dependent as the other person. Marriages sometimes end up like this; each spouse has no other relationships except for the other. They have complete dependence on each other. It seems to be fine until one member has to let go; then everything comes crashing down.

We are called to have healthy relationships, whether with our spouse, parents, children, or friends. Relationships in which we are free to engage and disengage at will. It is within this context that Jesus' comments in today's gospel are best understood. Jesus calls us to be free from our parents, children, or even friends, free to be in relationship with him.

Today and this week, may we examine our relationships with our parents, children, and friends and honestly determine if we are dependent on them or they are dependent on us in some unhealthy manner. As adults, it is time to stand up, let go, and be free for Christ.

Take My Yoke Upon You

When I go to visit the sick, in the hospital or in their homes, and celebrate the Sacrament of the Anointing with them, the gospel reading from today is the primary choice. At first, it seems strange that the church would choose such readings about taking a yoke upon them and learning from him. Haven't they got enough burdens already? Why ask them to take on more, even though it might be light? It seems to give little comfort to those in pain or near death.

Yet, if we examine these few words, we hear something different. We need to understand something about farming to fully appreciate this text. The yoke was a common wooden device, often hand-carved for specific animals, which paired two oxen together, making them a team. It is important to note that the work of the field did not change. However, because two oxen are now tied together, the work is easier but it is a team of two instead of one. The Lord invites us to tie ourselves to him so that he may share in our burdens of life and become part of our team. If we tie ourselves to him, then we will find relief in our suffering. Not so much that the pain will be lessened or disappear but because the Lord will be present with us, sharing it with us.

We believe as people of faith, that God is right here among us. God is here with us sharing in our joys and our sorrows. If only we could see his hand at work. If only we could believe, even when we do not see it. He promises, today and every day, that if we tie ourselves to him, we will feel our burdens lighten not because they are gone but because they are shared with our Lord. Our weariness and worries of life will lessen because the One who calls us to new life will be with us in all ways. How does this happen in real life? Where is God when our parent is suffering immensely with the last stages of cancer? Where is God when our son or daughter has lost their job again? Where is God when we suffer from ill-health? Where is God in the midst of the war and terror in the world? Where is God in this world torn with pain and strife?

As I tell the people anointed in the sacrament, their God is now present to them, in and through their family, who have gathered around their hospital bed. God is now present to them in the care and attention given to them through the nurses and doctors tending to their needs. God is now present to them through their friends who pray for them. God is present here and now. We will see and feel that reality if only we can take his yoke upon us. If we tie ourselves to him, then he will take us with him through the care and love of others.

Paul, in today's second reading to the Romans, reminds us to live in the Spirit of Christ and always remember that death is not the end. If we live in Christ, then we will die in Christ. We will share in eternal life, and death will have no power over us. If we can realise the gift of life that God offers through Christ's yoke, we can share in a Spirit-filled life, a Christ-centred life that anticipates the eternal reward promised to us all.

Today, may we choose to take on the yoke of the Lord and tie ourselves to him, the author of all life. May we know that in the midst of pain and struggle, we are the hands of God that stretch out to those in need.

15th Sunday in Ordinary Time
Isaiah 55:10-11; Psalm 65; Romans 8:18-23; Matthew 13:1-23

Enrich the Soils of Our Hearts Together

Last week in the *San Jose Mercury* newspaper, I read a story about jail gang DOs (Drop Outs). It was a powerful story about men, young and old, who are trying to put their lives together again. They are trying their hardest to turn their lives around. However, gang drop outs are at high risk in jails, because the gangs do not want anyone to leave. So, the county jail warden gives them special treatment and privileges, even assigning them a separate section of the jail, with extra protection. They need all the help they can get; turning around your life when you are a hardened criminal is a long and arduous task, with many setbacks. The gangs do not want them to succeed because if they do, more members will try to leave. However, this week, many former gang members did succeed in their first step. This week many graduated from High School and received their diplomas. Others are attending college level classes, and hope to graduate from college, too. Wow! What an achievement from inside the jail and against all odds. They are really turning around their lives and giving hope to so many others in the jail system.

In today's gospel, we hear that familiar parable of the sower and the seed. Here Jesus tells us that our hearts are like the soil. Depending on the readiness of the soil of our hearts, the seed of the Word of God will be received into our hearts and allow our lives to be forever changed by God's grace. Our work as disciples is to tend that soil and ensure that we have rich soil ready for planting.

The soil of the hearts of the prisoners in the county jail was very rocky. As gang members, their hearts were full of weeds. But now, they are turning over the soil of their hearts and trying to take the rocks out and pull the weeds. It is hard work, very hard work! It needs the best environment possible, like a protected section of the jail, to turn over this rocky and weed-filled soil.

We may not be hardened criminals, with severely rocky or weedy soil, but I think that we need to tend to the garden of our hearts. I think we need to spend some time, tilling the soil to ensure that we are ready for the seed of the Word of God. We may be strangled by the weeds of laziness in our spiritual lives and not tend to prayer on a daily basis. Maybe there are some rocks of unforgiveness, resentment, or jealousy and we cannot hear the loving, forgiving Word of God. Yes, I think we all have some work to till the soil of our hearts. This work of turning over our lives to God is called *conversion* and it requires a lot of hard work. It requires daily commitment to tend to the rocks and weeds of our hearts.

The other aspect of this parable is God's indiscriminate nature when it comes to giving his grace to humans. This aspect of the story shows us that God sows his seed or reveals his word *indiscriminately*. Like the sun and rain that fall on the weeds as well as the wheat, God does not distinguish among the recipients of his word. God's indiscriminate nature was manifest in the words and works of Jesus who reached out with the good news to *everyone* who would listen. The point of the mission for his disciples was to be in service to everyone.[1]

So too, we are called not only tend to our own gardens but to help others tend to their gardens. I do not mean that we tell others how weedy or rocky their soil is, but that we stand ready and willing to help when they decide to till their soil. Like the prisoners dropping out of gangs, people who are converting back to Christ need some protection from this often hostile world. They need some help in tilling their soil and at the very least they need some encouragement and instruction on the job of weeding or cleaning out the rocks. We all have weeds. We all have rocks. We all need to till the soil of our hearts. Today and this week, may we spend some time weeding and removing the rocks in the soils of our hearts; ready for the Word of God. May we also stand ready to create an environment for those around us who need the protection to start their process, too. Today, may we enrich the soils of our hearts, together.

---

1. Patricia Datchuck Sanchez, 'Celebration: An Ecumenical Worship Resource,' (Kansas City, Missouri: National Catholic Reporter Company, Inc, May 2005).

16th Sunday in Ordinary Time
Wisdom 12:13, 16-19; Psalm 86; Romans 8:26-27; Matthew 13:24-43

Potatoes of Pain:
Opportunities of Forgiveness

There is a story told of a young African woman who was captivated by the teaching and good works of some Catholic missionaries who came to their village many months earlier. However, the community was divided over their arrival. There was some disharmony among the different tribes. One Sunday, while leaving Mass, the young woman was stuck by a potato thrown by a fellow tribesman. He resented the presence of the missionaries in their village and any who had embraced these strangers among them.

The woman took the potato home with her and planted it in her back garden. She watered it often and months later it produced a rich harvest of potatoes. She then put some into a brown paper bag and sought out the man who had thrown the original potato and presented him with the new harvest.[1]

The young African woman embraced the new message she had heard preached about loving your neighbour and forgiving him. It seems so easy, but it is so hard to do. We often allow the hurts in our lives to determine our actions, reacting to what someone does to us with the same emotion returned to him. It is so easy to return hatred with hatred, or anger with anger, or not be friendly with those who are not friendly to us. At the very least, we pass it on to others. For example, we have a bad day at the office when our boss just dumps on us. We cannot do anything about it directly, so when we come home that night we dump on our spouse. Our spouse cannot do anything about our behaviour, so they dump on the children for not cleaning up or something. Then the children pass it on by dumping onto the dog! Or something like that! Yes, we are often content with passing on our frustrations, hurts, and anger. Instead, the gospel today challenges us to a new way of being. Instead, we are called to be yeast to make the bread around us; we are called to break the chain of negativity.

In today's gospel, we hear three different parables and they

---

1. Adapted from 'Connections' (Mediaworks, Londonderry, NH: July, 2005)

give different insights into Jesus' message. The first parable, as explained in the gospel, is about not judging others. To our ears today, allowing the weeds and the wheat to grow together may not seem like a big deal. But to the listeners in that agricultural setting in Jesus' times, this proposal would have sounded ludicrous and foolhardy. To allow the weeds to grow would have threatened the crop of wheat. It would have been considered crazy. However, this demonstrates the depth of God's forgiveness and willingness to allow us to return to his fold. If he is willing to allow everyone the opportunity to return to his fold, then his disciples must not judge others' lives. That is where the other two parables apply. Through the message of these parables, we are called to believe the potential of good in everything. We are called to be that mustard seed or be that yeast.

Like the young African woman, now a new disciple, we are called to turn every bad situation into goodness. We are called to turn our hurts and pains into goodness. That may sound easy but it is so hard. It is really hard work! That is why we come here each Sunday to this table, to receive strength for the week ahead.

When someone hurts us, our immediate response seems to be to hurt them back, or at the very least, pass that hurt onto someone else, albeit subconsciously. Today we are challenged to have the hurt stop with us. We are called to take the seeds of those hurts and pains and plant them in our hearts, tilling it with God's grace so that we can reap an abundant harvest of forgiveness and love. If we can do this, then we will be like the mustard seed, growing into a large plant for others to find shelter. If we can do this then we will be like yeast in our community, dispensing the love of Christ far and wide. This week, when we receive hurts and pains, may we choose to have them stop with us. May we turn those 'potatoes' of pain into opportunities for forgiveness and mercy. May we be the yeast for our community.

Remove the Clay
and let the Holy Spirit Shine

In 1957, a new highway was being constructed near Bangkok, Thailand. In order to complete the road, an enormous clay statue had to be moved. As the statue was being rigged up to be relocated, the workers accidentally cracked the clay image. A week of steady rain – not unusual in South East Asia – washed most of the clay away to reveal a statue of Buddha made of gold. Scholars believe that the giant Buddha was covered in mud to hide it from the Burmese invaders centuries earlier; in all probability, the invaders murdered the Thai monks who had covered the statue. Their secret remained hidden until the public work project in 1957. The priceless Buddha – weighing over 5,000 pounds – was installed in a specially built temple where it is revered today.[1]

As Christians we believe something sacred lies within each one of us, not an image of Buddha but the indwelling of the Holy Spirit. Yes, we believe that the Holy Spirit dwells deep within each of us, both in ourselves and in others. However, just like the 5,000lb golden image of Buddha hidden in clay, we often hide that image of God within us with false images. Sometimes, it is because we cannot handle the reality of God dwelling with us and it is easier to pretend that God does not exist. Sometimes, we do not like who we are or who we have become, and so we hide behind false images we construct. Other times, we protect our fragile internal images and hide our true selves from the potential ridicule of those who do not believe.

We are called to recognise that God lies within us, and to recognise that God dwells within every other person. Some of us find it is easy to recognise God in others but find it impossible to see God in ourselves. Others find it is easy to recognise God within us but find it hard to recognise God in others. Especially those we do not like, such as the family member we disagree with, or the office co-worker or neighbour who is unpleasant to be around, or the person across the world that terrorises others.

---

1. 'Connections' (Mediaworks, Londonderry, NH: July, 2005)

Some of us do a great job hiding that image of God within us with powerfully constructed images made of encased clay.

In today's first reading from the Book of Kings, Solomon is given the opportunity to ask God for anything and it will be granted him. Solomon asks for 'an understanding heart to judge [the] people and to distinguish right from wrong'. He does not ask for long life, wealth, or success over his enemies but he asks for wisdom to lead well the people of God in his tenure as king. And God grants it to him in abundance. We, too, ought to ask our God for a wise and understanding heart, so that we can see that image of God in ourselves and in others. We, too, ought to ask our God for the gift of wisdom to know right from wrong in all our endeavours.

If we seek such wisdom and understanding, then we can comprehend the gospel reading from today. The parables of the pearl of great price and the treasure found in the field are about people seeking the kingdom of God. We are called to be that people who seek that kingdom at all costs. We are called to be that people who sell all that we have for that wisdom. In other words, we are called to allow the old clay images of ourselves and of others to be destroyed, and the clear image of the Holy Spirit to shine forth.

I do not want to gloss over how difficult this project is. It is never easy to let go of the old images of ourselves or of others. It will require a commitment to remove the clay image and allow the destruction to take place. It will require a commitment to look at who we have become and to honestly admit that we have encased the Holy Spirit within us with other images. It will require an even bigger commitment to allow the images that others have of themselves to be destroyed. They, too, have encased the Holy Spirit in alternate images. Today and this week, may we take on this commitment and reflect on the image of God that dwells within us and others. May we break the clay of our old selves and allow the golden image of the Holy Spirit to shine forth.

Only a Quarter

There is a story told of a preacher from out-of-state who accepted a new assignment to a church in Houston, Texas. Some weeks after he arrived, he had an occasion to ride the bus from his home to the downtown area. After getting on the bus, he sat down and, looking at the change in his hand, he discovered that the driver had accidentally given him a quarter too much change.

As he considered what to do, he thought to himself, 'You'd better give the quarter back. It would be wrong to keep it.' Then he thought myself, 'Oh, forget it, it's only a quarter. It's not worth the extra trouble to chance falling on the bus. He probably doesn't even realise that he is missing a quarter. Who would worry about this little amount? Anyway, the bus company gets too much fare; they will never miss it. Accept it as a "gift from God" and keep quiet.'

When his stop came, he paused momentarily at the door, he reached into his pocket pulled out a quarter, handed it to the driver and said, 'Here, you gave me too much change.' The driver, with a smile, replied, 'Aren't you the new preacher in town?' 'Yes that's right; I am the new preacher,' responded the pastor. 'I have been thinking a lot lately about going somewhere to worship. I gave you an extra quarter as I just wanted to see what you would do if I gave you too much change. I guess I'll see you at church on Sunday.'

When the preacher stepped off of the bus, he literally grabbed the nearest light pole, held on, and said, 'Oh God, forgive me. I almost sold your Son for a quarter.'[1]

Every word, every action will tell others what we believe. This is a really scary example of how much people watch us as Christians and will put us to the test! If we are Christians, then our every word will carry as much weight as if God himself said it. Every single word and every single action is probably the only Bible some people will ever read today. We proclaim, by our actions and words, what we really believe.

Our lives are meant to be modelled after what Jesus did for us. Our lives are to be bread broken for others. Our lives are to be wine poured to others in service of them. We are called to

---

1. 'Connections' (Mediaworks, Londonderry, NH: March 2006)

serve others with every single word and action. And people are watching us, every Christian, not just the preachers, to see what we will do each day and each moment. Our actions will tell them if we really believe.

We might think that nobody really notices all the small things we do. Nobody is really watching us, so it does not matter if we are true to being a disciple at that moment. But they are watching every single action and word. It is all those little things that matter in our lives. If we are faithful in the little things, then we will be faithful in the larger things in life.

In today's gospel it is important to note that Jesus does not start his miracle from nothing. He starts from the small amount that the apostles offered him. They give what little they had – just five loaves and two fish – to Christ who blesses it, breaks it and gives it back to them to share. There was enough for all to have their fill and be satisfied. That's message for us.

We are called to share what little we have, our time, our talent, our treasure and offer them to Christ. Not that we give a huge amount but what little we give he will make great. He will bless it, break it, and give it back to us to share with others. There will be enough for all to have our fill and be satisfied. The little we share will turn into a miracle by God's action. We have to believe that if we do the little things right, then God will make those little actions into something great. By living out the Eucharist in little ways, we, with God, will make a huge difference overall.

By being kind and gentle to our children, especially if we need to correct them in some ways, by being kind and gentle to our parents, especially if they are ill or old, by being kind and gentle to the clerk at the grocery store or to the waiter at the restaurant. We have to find ways to be kind and gentle every day in our every single action and every single word because it is all being read as our living Bible.

We know that this task is so hard that we come to this table every week for further nourishment and strength as individuals and as a community, recognising that huge work starts in little places. We recognise at the beginning of Mass that we have failed in the past week and we recognise at the end of every Mass that we will try really hard to live it again this coming week. We come not only to taste and see the body and blood but we also leave here to be Christ to everybody we meet in every single word and action. It might the only Bible others read today and every quarter counts!

19th Sunday in Ordinary Time
1 Kings 19:9-13; Psalm 85; Romans 9:1-5; Matthew 14:22-33

Stealing a Moment of Silence!

Several years ago, I visited Kenya, Africa. I stayed in a parish right in the middle of the slums of Eldoret, the third largest city in Kenya. One Sunday, the parish youth group took me on a tour of their town. As we travelled around, we came to a small river where the only way across was a steel pipe about 2 feet in diameter. It was a windy day and I was a little nervous about crossing. All the kids were well on their way across before I could say anything. So I followed along! About half way across the river along this pipe, the wind blew against me and I smelled something strange. When I looked down at the water I realised for the first time I was crossing a river into which they pumped their raw sewage! I became terrified of falling in and the heat of the sun began to wear on me. I could not move any further! I could not move back or forward. My legs began to shake nervously. At first the kids laughed at me. And then they taunted me. Then they realised I was stuck. Eventually they made a human chain and pulled me in. I will never forget that experience because of the whiff of the river and the embarrassment of being frozen halfway across!

Sometimes in our lives, we start enthusiastically into some endeavour but somewhere along the way we lose faith in ourselves or in God. We doubt whether we can make it or not. Other times we discover something along the way that we had not bargained for and it all seems too much. We focus on the problems and it becomes overwhelming. Maybe it is a marriage that has gotten very difficult. Maybe it is school or work that now seems overwhelming. Maybe it is being a parent that is a little too much at times. Or maybe it is being a teenager where everything seems to be too boring! Somewhere along the line, we have felt overwhelmed.

In today's gospel, Peter starts out just fine crossing the stormy seas, but soon he, too, doubts and begins to sink. Here is the most trusted disciple of all, the church is to be built on Peter and he, too, doubts in a moment of weakness! He focuses only on the problem at hand and only sees the stormy seas. Instead of focusing on Jesus, he focuses on his problems. In desperation, he calls out to Jesus who reaches out and saves him.

In our own lives we sometimes reach the proverbial breaking point and we feel like we are sinking with the burdens of life. We can learn from Peter and cry out to the Lord for help. The question becomes: how do we do this in a meaningful way?

It seems to me that the first few lines of today's gospel give us a clue as to what the Lord suggests. It says that the Lord sends the crowds away and goes to the top of a mountain and prays. We need to get to know the Lord in prayer. I am not suggesting that we send our family and friends away and climb the nearest mountain. However, I think we need to spend some time, in silence, praying. We need to move to a place so we can hear the voice of God. As Elijah says, that 'whispering sound' that is his voice. God does not come in the earthquakes, winds, or fires but in a quiet whispering sound. We cannot hear that voice if we are surrounded by constant noise.

I know that many of you have children and life tends to be hectic with activity. Even our children take naps! We can steal a moment of silence with the Lord. Maybe it is driving in traffic with the radio off. Yes, we can steal some moments of silence in the middle of the day and spend it actively with God in prayer. We really need to learn to listen to that 'quiet voice' of God.

Authentically Invite People to the Table

In my home town in Ireland we had an exclusive golf club. Anyone who wanted to join had to put their name on a waiting list and some would wait 10-15 years. People would put their new born children on the list in the hope that they could be members by the time they were teenagers. But here is the real kicker – only members could put someone on the waiting list! Even to be on the waiting list, you had to know someone. I remember my friend becoming a member at age 22 and asking me if I wanted him to put me on the list. 'Don't worry,' he assured me, 'you'd only be 37 when you get in!' So, this year, I would have finally become a member of the exclusive club. I know many of you will think this is heresy, but I do not play golf, and the idea of waiting 15 years to be a member of anything seemed crazy to me. I declined my friend's offer.

There are a lot of clubs and organisations that exclude us from membership for different reasons. Some exclude on the basis of age or gender, some because of colour or race. Others accept only those who are wealthy or famous. Still others exclude people because of religion.[1]

Have you ever tried to join a group, club, or organisation and found yourself excluded because of who you are? Maybe it was a golf club, or sports organisation. Maybe it was professional or work related. Maybe it was a personal one. To be excluded because of who you are does not feel good.

In today's gospel, the Canaanite woman came to Jesus for help. She believed wholeheartedly in Jesus since she called him by the messianic title, 'Son of David.' But the disciples initially excluded her because she was not a Jew. They even asked Jesus to exclude her from their group! Indeed, Jesus rebuked her saying the same thing – that he had come to minister to the Israelites first and foremost. This reinforces the motif of Matthew's gospel – God's salvation is revealed to the world through the Jewish people. Jesus did not exclude as a personal insult but to affirm the reality of the salvation of all through the Jews.

---

1. Inspired by Patricia Datchuck Sanchez, 'Celebration: An Ecumenical Worship Resource,' (Kansas City, Montana: National Catholic Reporter Company, Inc, August 2002).

However, the Canaanite woman persists in her faith and argues with Jesus that even the dogs take scraps from their masters' tables. Jesus, impressed by her faith, heals her daughter and announces that the kingdom of heaven will be open to all who believe. In other words, we are all called to believe with such faith. We are all saved if we believe in Christ. After Jesus' death this message became abundantly clear. St Paul makes this known throughout the land by acknowledging that the Gentiles are also invited to salvation. In today's second reading, we hear Paul taunt his own Jewish people with this same message that all are saved. All nations and all people are invited to the table of the Lord, no matter who they are and where they come from. Sometimes I wonder if we really understand that message? All are welcome!

We are all called to welcome others to the table of the Lord. We are always called to invite others to the church. But to be authentic inviters to the table, we must be inclusive in our own lives. In other words, we need to open our exclusive groups to others. It may not be an official club or organisation but we have other groups that are exclusive! Our group of friends at school or work, our group of neighbours, our ethnic association, the group that we associate with either at work or church, even where or who we sit with at church. To be authentic in our invitation to this table, we must open up our friendships and families.

This week many schools will start back and one of the biggest challenges is to break up the cliques that form. Students often remain in those same groups all year. This week, can we teach our children and each other to invite people to the table by inviting people into our lives? We can welcome people in from the coldness of hostility and loneliness into the warmth of our friendships and our homes. We can open up ourselves to new friendships, invite the unwelcome relative to be part of the family again. I am not saying that this is easy but it is what we are called to do. Today and this week, we can be an example to our children and include others in our lives. By first inviting people into our lives and by being friends and neighbours to them, we can authentically invite them to the table of the Lord.

Practice What We Believe

In the last days of Communist rule in Poland, a visiting dignitary from the West was on a mission to Warsaw. A chief of protocol was assigned to accompany the official on his visit, which included attending Mass at the Cathedral. The visitor asked the Polish functionary, 'Tell me, are you a Catholic?' He replied quietly, 'Believing but not practising.' Then the diplomat said, 'You must a member of the Communist party?' The Polish official responded even more quietly, 'Practising, sir, but not believing.'[1]

We, as Catholics, are called to not only believe but to practise what we believe. We are also called to believe what we practise. While that may seem easy, it is actually not so easy to do. We all claim to believe and that is why we are here today. We want to practise and so we come here. That it is what today's gospel is all about – practising and believing the message of Christ.

In today's gospel, Jesus asks his disciples what others really say about him and if they really believe in him. Then he asks them what they believe. Peter gives the exemplar answer of a disciple, proclaiming Jesus to be the Son of the living God. Jesus knew that the disciples practised their faith and in particular Peter, who had walked with him since the beginning of his public ministry. Now he was asking if they really *believed* that he was the Son of God, the Messiah. After Peter restated his full faith in Christ, Jesus assures him that he will build the church upon him. Today, Jesus assures us that he will continue to build the church on his modern-day disciples – that is you and me, the People of God. And so, we are called to practise what we believe.

Each week, we come to this table and we proclaim what we believe. We say that we believe in one God, the Father, the Almighty. That he created heaven and earth, all that is seen and unseen.

Then we say that we believe in one Lord, Jesus Christ, the only Son of God, eternally begotten of the Father. We say that Jesus is the one true God, begotten, not made, one in Being with the Father. Through him all things were made. For our salvation, he came down from heaven: by the power of the Holy Spirit he

1. 'Connections' (Mediaworks, Londonderry, NH: August, 2005)

was born of the Virgin Mary, and became man. For our sake he was crucified under Pontius Pilate; he suffered, died, and was buried. On the third day he rose again in fulfilment of the scriptures; he ascended into heaven and is seated at the right hand of the Father. He will come again in glory and his kingdom will have no end.

Then, we say we believe in the Holy Spirit, who is the giver of life, who proceeds from the Father and Son. With the Father and Son he is worshipped and glorified.

Then, we say we believe in one holy, catholic, apostolic church. We acknowledge one baptism for the forgiveness of sins. We look for the resurrection of the dead, and life of the world to come.

Yes, every Sunday we proclaim our faith when we say the Nicene Creed. Sometimes, we say it so fast we underestimate the profundity of these words. Yet for centuries, people died for proclaiming such faith. The mere mention of belief in Jesus had people executed. We are truly blessed to live in a free society to be able to proclaim such belief and be able to live that reality in our lives. In today's letter to the Romans, St Paul is lamenting the lack of faith of his fellow Jews and their unwillingness to accept Jesus as the Christ. Yes, we come here to proclaim our faith in Jesus and then we ask for the nourishment to live that faith. We come to receive our daily bread in this church building so that we have the strength to practise the faith outside this church building and in our lives.

We practise our faith when we love our children who are sometimes little rascals, or most especially when they are little rascals. We practise our faith when we take care of our elderly parents who are no longer able to take care of themselves. We practise our faith when we are the first to forgive those people who have hurt us, intentionally or otherwise. We practise our faith when we dedicate ourselves to fighting for justice and speaking up for those who have no voice in their current circumstances. We practise what we believe when we live the gospel of Christ in the smallest ways in our daily lives.

Whether it is loving our children or parents, being the first to forgive, or speaking up for justice, we are called to practise what we believe because we are the church today. Upon us, Christ builds his church today.

22nd Sunday in Ordinary Time
Jeremiah 20:7-9; Psalm 63; Romans 12:1-2; Matthew 16:21-27

Be Ready to Turn Back

As many of you know, I just returned from a hiking vacation in the Colorado Rockies. Along with a friend and one of my brothers, we climbed several peaks that were 14,000 feet high. The beauty of these mountains lures you back again and again. Indeed, it feels like the peaks beckon you to come to the top. While the majesty of views from the peaks is magnificent, there are many challenges to these climbs. Because of the height of the mountains, the climate is such that by 1pm almost every day there are lightning and thunderstorms. To be safe, one needs to be up and off the mountain peaks by 12noon to avoid being struck by lightning. Sometimes, the weather can change rapidly and one needs to come down even before that time. It is a real danger and every year a number of people are struck, and killed, by lightning in the Rockies.

It sounds easy to leave when the dark clouds come in but sometimes it is very hard. Especially, when one has climbed for four hours and is only a half hour from the top with only a few hundred vertical feet to climb. It is very hard to simply turn around without 'peaking'. I am not sure what it is within us that says, 'Go ahead, you can make it!' It is some form of ego, I guess. We cannot seem to let go of it. When we set out to accomplish something it is hard to walk away, even though the signs tell us otherwise. We have a need to win, succeed, or be right. Even when within us a little voice is telling us to turn around. The common sense voice is warning us. We have the opportunity to listen and act right.

As we journey through life, I think the same thing happens to us. We set our minds on a task or action and we believe ourselves to be right. Then somewhere along the way, we get new information that tells we are on the wrong path or that things have changed and we need to adjust our path.

For example, I think this happens with spouses. We get into a discussion and we argue a certain point and then we become determined to win the argument. Somewhere in the conversation, we realise that we are now wrong and our spouse is right after all. What do we do? Nothing! We continue to argue the same way as if we had no new information. Yet, internally we know we are wrong.

The same thing happens when we are kids. Our parents ask us something and we exaggerate or tell a white lie. Then, we get into a discussion and we realise that we are really wrong to have lied. What do we do? Nothing! We often continue lying, getting ourselves into worse trouble. This happens to all of us.

Being ready to turn back and let go of our will or desire is the theme of today's readings. Paul, in his letter to the Romans, tells us that we are called to discern the will of God and not confirm ourselves to this age. We are called to listen to God and always do what is right, pleasing, and whole (perfect). We believe that God speaks to us in and through each other and we are called to listen to God in the voices of others.

But today's gospel goes one step further. We hear Jesus tell us that we must deny our very selves and follow in his footsteps. We have to lose our life to save it. We must let go of our own desire to be right, our need to achieve, our need to accomplish, and allow ourselves to be informed by God's will. We do that by listening to the wisdom of others and sometimes there is a price to pay for that action. The first reading from the prophet Jeremiah reminds us that we will often be persecuted for choosing to do the right thing. Jesus reminds us that we are called to carry that cross. If we choose to do the right thing then there will often be consequences for it. Sometimes, those consequences involve ridicule, but we must choose the right thing nevertheless.

Think of the times when we admit we are wrong in an argument and find ourselves being ridiculed for holding our previous position. Regardless of the consequences, it is still the right thing to do – admit when we know we are wrong. It is so hard to walk away when we are that close. So hard to admit that we are wrong in our current direction and change our minds to follow a new course set by the Lord through the advice of friends or family. No matter how close the peak of our mountain seems to be, we need to choose to turn back.

So whether we get into an argument with our spouse, or whether we tell some lies, or whether it be some other direction we set for ourselves, somewhere along the way we hear that little voice tell us to turn around and choose a new path. May we do the right thing – admit we are wrong and seek a new direction. Today, may we discern God's will by listening to others and be ready to change our minds.

23rd Sunday in Ordinary Time
Ezekiel 33:7-9; Psalm 95; Romans 13:8-10; Matthew 18:15-20

Early Warning System

One of the essential things we are learning from the Gulf Coast hurricane disaster is the importance of the early warning systems. We are learning about how much we knew in advance and how well we responded to this information. Everyone around the world knew forty-eight hours in advance about the possibility of a direct strike at the centre of New Orleans. Experts pretty much knew what to expect from a hurricane of this magnitude and the lethal blow it would give to the entire Gulf Coast. Indeed, the mayor of New Orleans had mandated a complete evacuation of the city and the governors of Louisiana and Mississippi had both declared a state of emergency, all thirty-six to forty-eight hours before the hurricane hit. As a result, hundreds of thousands of people had to move *en masse* to higher and safer places. Hundreds of thousands of people were saved.

I know that the media has focused on the people left behind, some because they could not move due to illness or disability; others because they thought they could ride it out; and still others because they choose not to listen. Many people were heroically saved in the days following and no doubt we will soon find out more reasons why so many were left behind.

Imagine, for a moment, if we did not have any weather forecasting. Imagine if we did not know that a hurricane was coming at all. Just one day it hit with all its force on the lands and the people of New Orleans, Louisiana, and Mississippi. Can you conceive how large the death toll there would have been? There would have been hundreds of thousands dead. There would have been incalculable human losses. It would have been even more horrific than what we now see.

While the early warning system will need improving, and I'm sure we will learn all about the mistakes made in ignoring certain obvious signs and signals, the current early-warning systems saved hundreds of thousands of lives throughout that region because so many people listened to the warnings.

In today's first reading, God is telling the prophet Ezekiel that he has appointed him as a watchman for his people. The Lord tells him that he is called to stand on guard for his people and save them, even from themselves. He tells Ezekiel that he will warn him and it is then his role and responsibility to inform the people of God's warnings no matter what the cost to himself. Indeed, he tells him if he does not prophesy as the Lord wants, then the blood of the evil people will be on Ezekiel's hands. No, he must stand and watch out for his people and warn them when they are in danger. That is the role of the prophet and the watchman.

In the second reading from the letter to the Romans, Paul, who is the exemplar disciple of Christ, acts as the prophet in this time, warning the Romans, and us, that if we do nothing else, we ought to love one another as we love ourselves since this one commandment sums up all the rest.

And in today's gospel, being the watchman and disciple are tied together in a unique way by Christ's example of resolving inevitable conflicts and divisions that arise. Jesus tells us that we love one another when we go first to the person with whom we are in conflict. Jesus tells us that we watch out for one another when we go and resolve our conflicts quietly with each other. If that does not work, then involve another person and if not then, involve the church community. Jesus tells us the way we love one another is by correcting each other quietly and respectfully. We are called to be the early warning system for each other in our community. This is the way of the watchman or prophet.

This is not too difficult with someone over whom we have authority or power, like our child, younger sibling, or employee. It is quantifiably more difficult when the role is reversed. That is when we need a lot more courage and strength. For example, when the child corrects the parent or the employee has to correct the boss. Imagine for a moment your daughter coming to you, saying, 'We need to sit and talk for a moment. You need to understand that over the last few weeks, you have been stressed out and acting very inappropriately, in particular towards us, your children. So, you are now on a time-out. Think about what you have been saying to us and how you have lost your temper with no reason.' Wow! That would take a lot of courage indeed! Or if we said something similar to our boss about how they have been treating another employee in some inappropriate manner. Yes, it would take the courage and strength of a prophet to do so.

But that is exactly what we are called to do when one of us is acting wrongly. We are called to watch out for one another and be the prophet for our wrong behaviours. We are called to be courageous and be like a watchman. Now I do not mean for you, boys and girls, to go to your parents and tell them how 40 hours of television is simply not enough and endless hours on the computer games is most appropriate. No, I am talking about some seriously wrong behaviour that is damaging to them or to us. I mean speaking up for an unjust situation at the office. I mean being willing to take a stand for something righteous. And this requires courage.

The other possibility is that we need to be corrected for some behaviour of our own. If this is the case, then we need to be open and give permission to others, allowing them to correct us. Spouses do this well for one another about minor issues but often fail when it comes to major issues. It is hard to be open to a major correction of our own behaviour. But when it is done in a loving way we can succeed.

So today and this week, may we have the courage to be a prophet or watchman in the midst of our families, friends, and offices and not be afraid to challenge the unjust action. Or better still, may we open ourselves for the loving correction of others. May we be attentive to the early warning system and be ready to act appropriately.

Concrete of Pain

When walking in the neighbourhood the other day, I saw a man working in his garden mixing concrete with a shovel. After he was done setting the concrete, he cleaned the shovel with water, washing away all the wet concrete. I think this is a perfect metaphor for life.

We go through our daily life living as best we can, yet we often experience pain and hurt. Living life is mixing the concrete; the wet concrete left on the shovel is the pains and hurts we gather along the way. The action of washing the wet concrete from the shovel is forgiving the hurts and those who have caused them. If we choose not to wash away the concrete while it is still wet, it is unforgiveness and it hardens over time. Oftentimes it hardens so well that it encases our hearts in stone.

I remember when I was a child my father had a shovel he used to mix concrete but he rarely washed it off. Every time he would use the shovel he would raise it high and smack it hard on the ground, breaking off a lot of the concrete but not all of it. Over time that shovel became encased in concrete and soon it got so heavy that it was impossible to use at all. When he got a new shovel he ensured that we washed it every time. If we forgive as soon as someone hurts and betrays us, then the concrete of pain has no chance to harden our hearts. However, if we wait too long, then it hardens and our hearts become heavy and burdened.

In today's gospel, Peter asks Jesus how often does he need to forgive his offenders, how often does he need to wash away that concrete of pain: As many as seven times? Jesus says not seven but seventy-seven times. In other words, every time a person offends us we are called to forgive them. Seventy-seven is the biblical way of saying 'every time.' Peter must have been devastated to hear that answer. He thought he was a great disciple, telling Jesus that he forgives his enemies as many as seven times. But Jesus raises the bar and says we are to forgive every time. We are to forgive and wash away that pain and hurt while it is still 'wet concrete' and fresh enough to wash away, before it hardens within our hearts. Then Jesus gives us the motivation to do so. We are forgiven first by our God in heaven and therefore we should forgive others their hurts to us. Jesus illustrates this lesson with a powerful example of the king who forgives the debt of a servant's large loan and how that same servant wrangled a small debt from a fellow servant – a powerful lesson indeed. The wise teacher of students in Jerusalem, Sirach, in the first reading says much the same thing. We need to forgive because we have been forgiven first.

Oh, that is so easy to say but we all know how difficult it is to do. Hurts and pains affect us on different levels. When someone calls us a name, it hurts us but we are usually able to get over it. But when someone whom we have loved, especially a parent, spouse, child, sibling, or friend, wounds our very person, it penetrates deep into our hearts and causes significant pain. That type of wound is so difficult to forgive. It is so hard to wash away that hurt. It seems easier to hold onto that concrete of pain because it seems to protect us from further harm. In reality, it hardens our hearts and we become burdened greatly.

On a different level, we can experience hurt as a community. Some years ago, we, as a nation and as a community of Americans, experienced one such deep wound when the World Trade Centers and Washington were attacked. That wound still runs deep in many people's hearts and the concrete is beginning to harden. Yes, as a community and as individuals, we experience hurt. The temptation is to let the concrete of pain harden and remain unforgiving towards anyone who hurts us.

Real concrete takes only a few hours to fully harden. Our pain and hurts take longer to harden. For us, that is our opportunity to wash away the pain by forgiving the hurt done to us, and those who have done it. May we, as a nation, take this opportunity to forgive, from our hearts, those who have hurt and injured us. Also may we, as individuals, take this opportunity to forgive those who have personally hurt us. It is not easy to do but that is our mission.

If we have some old grudge or unforgiveness in our hearts, and the concrete is already hard, then maybe we can ask God to smash the concrete and set us free from our heavy and burdened hearts. In all the new hurts and pains we may receive this week, may we wash it away immediately and with God's grace not allow any to harden for long. This week may we forgive because we were forgiven first and not allow the concrete of pain to harden.

Pregnant With Salvation

For my thoughts are not your thoughts
and my ways are not your ways, says the Lord (Is 55:8)

A friend of mine recently told me that his wife was pregnant. Delighted for him and his wife, I congratulated him and got all excited for them. Trying to calm me down, he said, 'She's only a little bit pregnant!' 'A little bit pregnant!', I said, 'What does that mean? Either she is pregnant or she is not!' Of course, I understand that he was trying to tell me, that there was a long way to go for full term, and it might be precipitous to celebrate. It reminds me of someone who remarked of his wife, 'She's almost pregnant.' Almost! Now hang on a minute! Either you are pregnant or not!

I think pregnancy and salvation are a lot alike. Either you are saved or you are not. There is no 'almost saved' or 'a little bit saved'. If we were a little bit saved, then which part of us is saved? No, we are completely saved. When Jesus Christ died on the cross and rose from the dead, he guaranteed salvation for all of humanity. Either we are saved or we are not. Jesus tells us that we are all saved and all we have to do is accept that offer of salvation.

Today's gospel is about salvation, and God's promises. Jesus gives us a very powerful and provocative story about an extraordinarily generous landlord of a vineyard, and his treatment of the day workers who come so late in the day. This represents the end times and how God will give entry into the kingdom of God to anyone who comes to him, even at the last minute. The story is about salvation and not economics. This is not about how to run a business. If anyone actually ran a business in that manner, he or she would soon be out of business. Although there is a temptation to preach about social justice, today's gospel readings are about the eschaton – the end times. It is about the incredible generosity of our God and his boundless mercy and forgiveness. He offers, to all of humanity, the gift of salvation and it is up to us to accept or reject it. St Paul refers to this reality in his letter to the Philippians, assuring them that human life is transformed in Christ, not to worry about death as it gains us eternal life: 'For to me life is Christ, and death is a gain.' Yes, salvation is ours for the receiving and our lives are an opportunity to live out that reality.

One thing I know, pregnant women have a great affinity for other pregnant women. I mean, two pregnant women can be in a crowded room and somehow they will find each other and start to talk about their pregnancies. They will chat and share stories with each other, assuring one another of the value of the life that grows within. They would never look at another pregnant woman and say, 'What! You are also pregnant. I cannot believe it!' Or never talk to them and not encourage them. Such a thing is inconceivable. Pregnant women would not be jealous of other pregnant women. No, instead they rejoice with all pregnant women and share the joy of giving birth to new life.

The same ought to be true for us who are pregnant with salvation. We are all pregnant with that Spirit who gives us eternal life. We ought not to be jealous about another person who has just gotten pregnant with salvation, accepting the message of Christ for themselves. Instead, we rejoice that they have heard the call and responded with open hearts to conversion.

I know it is difficult to understand that reality. It is difficult for us, who claim to live the gospel, to rejoice when a bad person, a murderer, suddenly seems to have found Christ in their lives. It doesn't seem fair that someone who has never lived a good life till the very last few moments of their lives should get the same treatment as those who have lived the gospel all their lives.

But God's ways are not our ways. God's way opens salvation to all who wish to receive it. God's salvation is 'an all or nothing deal'. We cannot be partially saved or almost saved. We are fully saved by Christ's death and our task is to openly receive that gift. We might not want it fully but God offers it fully to us.

Yet, it is no easy task to accept this gift. There are many in this world who will hear the call and choose to not receive and, indeed, reject God's offer. For those, we are truly saddened. For the rest of humanity who are willing to say yes, even if it is at the last minute, we rejoice wholeheartedly. We give thanks to God for the free gift of salvation at this table each week and try to live that reality. As St Paul tells the Philippians, 'conduct yourselves in a way worthy of the gospel of Christ' (1 Cor 1:27a). We have received the gift of being pregnant with salvation. It is our responsibility to bring it to full term.

My Final Answer

There is a popular television game show called 'Who Wants To Be a Millionaire?'[1] The contestants compete for the coveted prize of $1,000,000 by choosing between four possible answers to a question. At first, the questions are easy and the contestants advance rapidly. Then the questions quickly become difficult, requiring them to ponder the answers carefully. Often they talk through their answers with game host, Regis Philbin, vacillating between the four possible answers. When they choose their answer, Regis asks them, 'Is that your final answer?' And they answer, 'Yes that is my final answer!' If they are right they continue on to the next round and a continued shot at the one million dollars. If they are wrong, they go home.

On our journey through life, we encounter many questions and we talk through the possible answers with neighbours, family, friends, and even with God. But in the end our 'final answer' comes not from what we say we will do, but from what we *actually* do. Our final answer is our actions.

In today's gospel, we hear Jesus give a scenario of two sons who were asked to work in the vineyard. One promised he would not do so and then changed his mind and did so. The other promised he would and then changed his mind and did not do so. Their final answer is what they *actually* did.

In the first reading, God also speaks through the prophet Ezekiel, stating the same thing about his judgement of sinners. His judgement will be based on their final actions, correcting a view of predestination of sinners and saints alike. The Israelites of old believed in double predestination – those whose ancestors were evil were damned and those whose ancestors were good were blessed. God changed that misunderstanding in the Old Testament through the prophet Ezekiel and in the New Testament through Jesus. We always have the opportunity to turn away from sin. We always have the opportunity to turn back towards God. We see that we will be judged not on what we claim or on what we say we will do but on what we *actually* do.

---

1. Patricia Datchuck Sanchez, 'Celebration: An Ecumenical Worship Resource,' (Kansas City, Missouri: National Catholic Reporter Company, Inc., September 2005).

One important thing about today's gospel is the way in which the sons changed their minds. One changed his mind for the good and did what the father had asked. He had a conversion of heart. The other changed his mind for the bad and failed to do what he had promised. What is it within us that enables us to change our minds? How do we move from not doing good to doing good? One place to start is by reflecting on our actions and reflecting on what we say we will do. Then we have to talk with our friends and family about those decisions, seeking their wisdom and maybe even seek direction from God in prayer. Often, our own reflections bring us to a different action than what we originally set out to do. We change our minds and that change is a good thing. Like the contestants in the game show, we talk our options through, seeking the right answer. Our final answer will be in what we *actually* do.

Sometimes it is very hard to change our minds. It is hard to admit our mistakes and move in a different direction. So what tools do we have to help us in this manner? One of the things that Irish Catholics, indeed all Catholics of old, are famous for is the use of 'guilt' to change our minds. We were often shamed into doing things we did not want to do, or we felt guilty if we did not do as 'Father,' or 'Sister' asked.

First, I want to distinguish between healthy and unhealthy guilt. Healthy guilt motivates us to do what is right and to not do what is wrong, morally or otherwise. Unhealthy guilt is neurotic and locks us into a never-ending analysis of possibilities, often ending in lack of action in any way. I want to talk about the healthy guilt, which enables us to do good and avoid evil. If we allow ourselves to reflect upon our actions in a healthy way and feel guilt therein, then we will be motivated to do good and see the positive consequences of our actions. At the same time, we will see the harm we could do and thus avoid the occasions of evil.

When we come to this table each week, we proclaim our faith in Jesus and his work. We say we believe in him and his way for us. But our final answer is not here at this table. Our final answer is when we leave here and go into our homes and offices and live in the world out there. Our final answer is what we *actually* do. Today, as we leave here, what will be our final answer? No matter what comes our way, may we always choose Christ and his way.

27th Sunday in Ordinary Time
Isaiah 5:1-7; Psalm 80; Philippians 4:6-9; Matthew 21:33-43

No Weeds Is Not Enough

The US Department of Agriculture recently determined that the cost of raising a child in America is somewhere between $9,250 and $10,300 per year. The American Life Institute determined that the average family will spend somewhere in the range of $190,000[1] on each child from conception to age 18. And, those numbers do not include private tuition fees for elementary, high school, or college! Is that all there is to raising a child? I mean if we give $190,000 over 18 years, are we done? We know that a child cannot survive on food, water, or shelter alone. There is more to raising a child than the bare essentials. Every child needs to feel loved and cared for. Admittedly, we do that through caring for their basic needs. But there is much more than mere economic terms. Every child not only needs love but we have to teach them how to love others, too. These are the most important aspects of child rearing – loving them and showing them how to love others.

Let me give you an illustration. If I said today that I had a garden with absolutely no weeds, what would you say? You would say it must have taken a lot of hard work; it is nearly impossible to believe; or I must spend a lot of time in the garden; or I might not be telling the whole truth. What if I then told you that I have no flowers or plants in my garden? I have nothing, no weeds, no flowers, fruits or vegetables either! You might say that it is not much of a garden, that it is not much use, that it is a strange thing to have a garden without any produce. You would be very right. For what purpose would a piece of land be if it is only bare? It has no weeds, but it produces nothing else either!

Well, I think, as Catholic Christians, we often resign ourselves to having gardens with no produce. We spend endless amounts of time ensuring that there are no weeds in our garden: that we do not sin and we avoid evil. And that is great. But if we have no flowers, no plants, no produce, what is the point of the garden? We need to do more than avoid evil and sin. We need to do some good works. We need to grow some produce!

---

1. Patricia Datchuck Sanchez, 'Celebration: An Ecumenical Worship Resource,' (Kansas City, Missouri: National Catholic Reporter Company, 27 Ordinary A, October 2, 2005).

In today's gospel, and in the first reading from the prophet Isaiah, we hear about a vineyard and its owner coming to collect the produce from the tenants. They either refuse to grow anything or refuse to hand it over. The tenants refuse to work the vineyard as it was designed. Jesus is trying to tell the religious leaders of his time that there is more than avoiding sin and evil, they need to produce good fruit. And the vineyard is not theirs but the Lord's.

We are reminded that each of us has been given a piece of the vineyard of the kingdom of God. Each of us shares in that kingdom within ourselves. Each of us has been given the responsibility to produce good fruit for that kingdom. We are reminded that it is not enough to avoid evil and sin; we need to produce real fruit from our labours. It is not enough to have no weeds in our garden, we need to have some plants that produce fruit or nourishment. It is not enough to give our children food and water, we need to show them love and how to love others.

There are many ways in which we can produce good fruit, but all ways require of us a huge commitment. Having a garden full of fruit-producing plants is hard work. But that is our commitment to being Christians. We first start with our family and friends but we do not stop there. It is not enough to avoid our family member who has hurt us; we may need to stretch out in reconciliation. It is not enough to avoid that person who we do not like at work, school, or in the neighbourhood but we may need to extend a fresh hand of hospitality. It is not enough to just give money to charities. To those in need we may need to get involved in fighting for justice. Whether it be with a family member, or friend, or victim of the Gulf Coast disasters we are called to produce good works and not just avoid evil. This week, may we look at the gardens of our lives and not only make sure there are no weeds but ensure there is some good fruit growing as well.

Open Seating in Heaven

Years ago when Southwest Airlines was new they were known as the 'no-frills' airline because their prices were hard to beat. They always get you there on time, cheaply. While they have changed the reservation system, the problem back then was seating was on a 'first-come, first-serve' basis. Nobody could reserve seats. If you want a decent seat, you need to get to the airport very early. On one occasion, I was at the airport for a Southwest flight nearly three hours before the departure time. I was sure I would get a seat number assignment below 10. You can imagine my shock when I received ticket number 76! Not only did I not get the top ten, but also I did not even make the first seating. I mean, do people have no lives that they can get to the airport three hours before the flight leaves?

Back then, if we were to travel on other airlines we could be guaranteed a seat when we purchase the ticket because we have reserved seating. Indeed, if we want, we can get first class reserved seats. No matter what, we have reserved seats. There is no need to hurry to the airport; we will get the reserved seat no matter what time we arrive. When it comes to the departure time, passengers are welcomed on board by their seat assignment. First Class passengers are welcomed on board first. If you have ever travelled First Class you will know the pleasure of being ushered on with dignity.

This is the scenario Jesus is trying to illustrate in today's gospel parable of the king and the wedding feast. The Israelites believed they had reserved seating when it came to the kingdom of God. The scribes and elders thought they had First Class seats. They believed they did not need to worry, because they had a guaranteed place in eternal life, and their practice was rooted in that presumption. Jesus comes along and warns them that there are no longer any reserved seats. The kingdom of heaven now has only open seating. It is open to all and everyone who accepts the invitation. Just because we have the invitation does not guarantee a seat.

You can imagine how difficult that was for them to hear. Indeed, it is not so easy for us to hear either. I think we, too, have adopted a somewhat similar attitude. Most of us believe that because we are decent Catholics and because we come to church regularly we will get admitted into the kingdom of heaven. Most of us also find it hard to stomach, that people who have not lived a good life and convert at the last moment of their life will also get admitted into the kingdom of heaven. Most of us find that hard to take. Here we are coming to church every week and trying to live a good life but we get no better seat than those who have lived it up for their whole life. It does not seem fair, does it?

The last words of the gospel today are also important: 'Many are invited but only few are chosen.' We know from our tradition that God came to save all of humanity and therefore all have received an invitation. But only a few have accepted the offer to come to the table. We ought to celebrate the gift that we all have received. We ought to celebrate that we received an invitation. We ought to celebrate that there is open seating because we now have a seat, as long as we accept the offer. The real task of a disciple is to fully accept the invitation.

Here is the rub! When we become disciples, we have significant responsibilities. When we accept the offer to come to the table of the Lord, then we accept the responsibility of being a disciple in the world. Remember the man who was kicked out of the reception because he was not wearing a wedding garment? It seems unfair to treat him so. After all, he did come in from the 'main streets' and did not have much time to prepare for a party. However, we need to understand this passage a little more. A wedding garment was a garment very much like this chasuble that I am wearing for today's Mass. The garment went over one's other clothes, more like robe that covered everything else. It was the custom at that time for the host of a wedding party to supply wedding garments at the door on the way in. So, to not wear a wedding garment at a wedding, one would have to refuse to wear the supplied garment. It would have been a direct snub to the host.

When we were baptised, whether as a child or as an adult, we were given a light, symbolising the light of Christ. We were also clothed in a white garment, symbolising the garment of Christ. We promised to always wear that garment by choosing to live as a disciple. When we accept the invitation to come to the feast, then we also accept the challenge of putting on the garment of Christ. What does that look like? It means when someone hurts us profoundly and we want to react by hurting him or her in return or seeking revenge in some way, that we put on the garment of Christ and allow Christ to heal us and enable us to forgive that person. It also means that we reach out to those who are hurting. Maybe it is stretching out to someone who is disenfranchised by our institutional church in some way, whether it is a divorced person or a gay person. We are called to stretch out to them and let them know that no matter what, they also have an invitation to the Lord's Table.

Yes, we are called to put on the garment of Christ when we come to this table on Sunday; we are also called to keep that garment on all week. It is not enough to just come to this table on Sundays; we must live the liturgy in our lives by wearing that garment of Christ. There is only opening seating in the kingdom of heaven. May we live the gospel by putting on the garment of Christ.

God's Currency

If I said the word 'peso' what would come to mind? Mexico. If I said 'yen' then Japan would come to mind. If I said 'euro' then Europe would come to mind. And of course, if I said 'dollar' then United States of America would come to mind. That is because these are the currencies, the monetary systems of those countries, through which we deal, whether it be goods or services. We cannot spend the peso in Europe or the yen in Mexico. Instead, we need to exchange that currency for the national one, so that we can do business in that country. Each country has its own monetary system and that currency is only valued in that country. Although we can exchange it for local currency, it does not always have the same value. On nearly every currency in the world, the Head of State, or a former Head of State appears on the currency. This is an indication that a particular currency belongs to a particular country.

The tradition of putting the Head of State on the currency has been around a long time. In today's gospel, we hear how the Roman currency had Caesar's head and inscription on all coins. But Jesus' answer is more than a monetary lesson. It is more than an avoidance of their trick question about the separation of church and state. It is, instead, a profound answer to the question of life itself. If we are to give to Caesar what is Caesar's – his currency, and give to God that which is God's, then the question that begs to be answered is, 'What is God's currency?'

We might initially say that it is forgiveness, truth, compassion, faith, hope, and love. All of those truly reside in God in the fullest sense. But when we think of a currency, we need to remember that it is made and owned by that nation, and at some point it is returned to that nation or state. In other words, it is created by some treasury and at some stage it returns to that treasury. What does God create that will always return to him? Yes, human beings.

Humans are God's currency, his created treasure, and when our time is up we return to his treasury in heaven. Unlike a regular currency, with only an image of the Head of State, we are created in his image, and not only his image, but his very self dwells within us in the form of the Holy Spirit. A $20 bill always has a $20 value until it returns to the treasury. No matter how old or new, tattered or torn, marked or dirty it gets, its value always remains $20. So too, it is with us. Every human being is created with an unchangeable value until the day we return to his heavenly treasury. Each and every human, no matter where we were born, how old or young, how broken or polished, how dirty or sinful, all have value in God's eyes. We are his currency.

The question we need to ask ourselves then is 'How well do we spend God's currency?' How well do we spend ourselves? Just like monetary currency, we define ourselves by the way we spend our money. If we buy beautiful, smart-looking clothes, but do not take care of the body that it covers, then that will define us. If we spend all our time at the office earning money for our family, but have no time to spend with our family, then that will define us. If we buy a magnificent house, but cannot afford the food on the table, or are incapable of giving the love to make it 'home', then that will define us. Maybe that definition is not what we had hoped.

In the same manner, the way we spend ourselves will define us. If we spend all our time serving only the needs of our children and have no time for anyone else, then that will define us. If we spend all our time serving others and have no time for our family, then that will define us. We need to seek the balance between serving ourselves and serving others. It seems today that we serve our children's every desire. We shuttle them from one event and activity to another. We enroll them in one sport after another, and keep them and ourselves so busy that we hardly have any time for family, not to mention others outside the family. Then there are those of us who serve others all the time and have little or no time for our own family. Yes, we are called to serve others but we need to seek balance. We are called to spend ourselves for others. That requires us to take care of our currency so that it will last a lifetime.

This week may we understand that our challenge is to spend ourselves, God's currency, for others and give to God what is God's.

Love is a Decision

Mark Twain is purported to have said, 'It's not what I don't understand about the Bible that bothers me, but what I do understand.'[1] If there is ever a section of the Bible to which this statement applies, it is this passage from the gospel of Matthew: 'the greatest commandment is to love our God with all our heart, all our soul and all our mind. The second commandment is to love our neighbour as ourselves.' Yes, we understand this passage all right, but living it is not so easy. It is very difficult to practise in real life. Where do we start for the genuine practice of love?

A few years ago, I attended a Retrouvaille Programme weekend. For those who do not know, this is a programme for those experiencing deep trouble in their marriages. It is often the couples' last effort to keep their marriage together. As you can imagine, it can be a very intense scenario when you get thirty such couples together. Fundamentally, it is a peer ministry where three couples, along with a priest, share their experience in a very structured format, using a model that has worked for many decades. It has a phenomenal success rate, keeping over 85% of marriages together after the weekend.

One of the cornerstone sessions of the weekend is called 'love is a decision'. The focus of the session is on the decision itself, and how loving can be hard work. Most of us who attended the weekend had heard this phrase before but we had never understood it in that way. It makes a lot of sense, but we rarely think of love in this manner – love is a decision.

The reality of any married life is that there are good days and not so good days. There are days when you wake up, and look over at your spouse and say something like: 'Oh, I am the luckiest person in the world.' Then there are days when you look over at your spouse and wonder what happened, how you got here with this spouse! Yes, there are good and not so good days; but every day we have a choice and a decision to make. I know that many of you thought it was a decision made once at the altar on your wedding day. In reality, it is a decision you need to

---

1. Jude Siciliano OP, 'Preachers Exchange: Ordinary 30A Reflections' (Raleigh, NC: preachex@opsouth.org).

make every day. You choose to love your spouse each and every day. That is also true for your children, your parents and your friends. You make a decision to love them every day. Some days are easier than others, but it is your decision.

Jesus goes a little further than this decision to love others. He tells us this decision starts with loving ourselves first. I really believe that this is where most of us trip up. It is hard to genuinely love ourselves for who we really are and not who we would like to be. When we look in the mirror in the morning and see how we are getting old, with our greying hair and new wrinkles marking our wear. We see how we cannot move, or do things as we used to. Maybe, we just would like to look different, a different nose, cheek, or chin line, or less weight, overall. That is just the physical body we see. We, then, look a little deeper and see how much more we'd like to change. How we walk or talk, or maybe a habit we cannot seem to break. Yes, when we look in the metaphorical mirror, it is sometimes very hard to accept what we see. Yet, that is exactly where Jesus has us start. We need to not only accept but love ourselves just the way we are, with all our imperfections and inadequacies, as well as all our gifts and talents.

We cannot genuinely love others if we cannot love ourselves. Instead, we will love them in some self-serving way, in order that they love us back, or give us the love we cannot give ourselves. Jesus has us start by authentically loving ourselves. If we can only accept and love ourselves with our imperfections and inadequacies as well as our gifts and talents, then we will be able to love others with their imperfections and inadequacies as well as their gifts and talents. We will love others for who they are – a child of God. That is really hard work and we know it. But that is where it all starts – with ourselves. Today and this week, may we hear God's commandment and make that decision to authentically love ourselves, with all of our imperfections and inadequacies. Today, we choose Christ and we choose love.

Wristband of Christ

A cluster of students once huddled together outside the university's main building on a cold winter day, smoking cigarettes to their hearts content. One of them extended his arm to light the other's cigarette, revealing from beneath his coat cuffs and sweater, a bright yellow wristband engraved with the words *LiveStrong* – this is the motto of the Lance Armstrong Foundation.[1] The bracelets, sold at $1 apiece, have raised more than $55 million for cancer research. Somehow, the students missed the contradiction of their actions. Here they are demonstrating their support for cancer research by wearing the yellow wristband, while with the same hand, smoking cigarettes, possibly causing cancer in their lungs. Their actions are a contradiction!

Our lives, too, are filled with many such contradictions. Maybe some of us have recently attended a sports game with children. Oftentimes, there is some strange behaviour from parents on the sidelines, becoming enraged at the officials over some minor play. They use colourful language and gestures, demonstrating everything we ask our children not to do.

Many of us have home exercise equipment. They are great for holding our clothes, or just lovely furniture to look at. But are rarely being used for exercise! Another contradiction to what we claim.

Or my personal favourite: someone cuts us off on the road while driving, and as they pass, they offer some words of advice with gestures to match. The only problem is: those words aren't so kind and the gestures are not exactly hands waving. Then, as the car speeds by, you see rosary beads hanging from the rearview mirror, or a bumper sticker saying 'Go Jesus'. Yes indeed, go Jesus! What a contradiction!

Yes, life is full of contradictions; some are funny while others are deadly. In today's first reading, we hear from the prophet Malachi, who scolds the priests for living a contradiction. They were not living their faith and consequently leading the people

---

1 Story rephrased from 'Connections' October 23, 30th Sunday of the Year (Mediaworks, Londonderry, NH: October 2005).

astray. In the gospel, we hear Jesus admonish the Pharisees and scribes for holding to a strict interpretation of the Law for others, while they themselves do not uphold the Law. They do not practice what they preach. Actually, they worked out laws and observances, 613 in all, that were burdensome to the vast majority of ordinary people, but they also worked out clever loopholes to these laws, so that they wouldn't apply to themselves. Jesus accuses them of being hypocrites, living a contradiction.

When we hear these scripture readings, with admonishment of the leaders of that time, it is easy to join in and complain about our leaders. We have plenty of problems with our political leaders who seek to use their office for personal gain. We know there is corruption in our businesses, with a leader cashing in before the company goes belly up. We have plenty of problems with our own religious leaders who did not act as they could or should have. We want our political, business, and religious leaders to be held to a high standard and rightly so, but that does not take us off the hook. You see, Jesus would consider every one of us leaders. We are leaders by our Christian baptism. We are called to lead all people to a better way of living. We are called to live the gospel at all times.

We need to examine our own lives and see what our 'wristbands' are. Do we live some contradictions of our own? Do we tell our children or parents not to do a particular thing, and then find ourselves doing that very thing? Do we tell our spouses not to say things a certain way, and then find ourselves saying things exactly that way? Do we share with our friends or co-workers about how wrong it is to gossip, and then find ourselves conversing about someone? Yes, there is a lot of contradiction in our own lives too. We are called to change our actions. We are called to be consistently good, in both word and deed.

Today's gospel continues from last week's, telling us that the greatest commandment is to love our God with all our heart, all our soul, and all our mind. The second commandment is to love our neighbour as ourselves. We know how hard a choice this is to live. Jesus admonishes the Pharisees and the religious leaders for not living the words they preached. May we hold, not only our leaders, but also ourselves accountable, to live what we preach in our own lives, with our children, parents, spouses, friends, and co-workers. May we love others in word and action. May we live without contradiction.

Apprentice of Christ

I am not sure if you have ever seen the television programme *The Apprentice*, a weekly show about a group of people competing to become an apprentice of Donald Trump. The contestants are divided into two teams and are given a task to complete. The losing team ends up in the boardroom and one of the team is 'fired'. By process of elimination one person becomes the apprentice.

Last week's show was an epic one. The task was to create a marketing event to help increase the sales at one of these sports megastores. The first team chose to create a marketing event around golf and created a miniature golf course inside the store. As people played through the golf course they were solicited for sales of all sorts of golf accessories and apparel. The team clearly enjoyed themselves and did very well, increasing sales by over 74%.

The other team chose a similar approach and created a marketing event around baseball. They also created a miniature baseball field and positioned the baseball goods around the field. But then they decided to put a full-size batting cage in the centre of the field. You can imagine how a batting-cage would dominate this miniature baseball field, and it did. It was a full-scale attraction and people lined up to bat in the cage. The team got carried away with helping each of the customers learn how to bat correctly. The team was so busy having fun they completely lost focus on the task in hand. In the end, not only did they not increase sales but they actually decreased sales by 35%. Wow! What a total disaster!

When Donald Trump sees them in the boardroom, he is totally ticked off, as they completely failed. He scolded them for completely missing the point: the goal was to increase sales and they completely lost focus. He considered the entire team idiots and fired all of them for their lack of performance.

I think today's gospel is very similar to this story. Jesus tells us that if we miss the point, we too, are fired! In the gospel, Jesus is the bridegroom, and you and I, as disciples, are the bridesmaids. Whether we are wise or foolish will depend on our ability to keep our focus. That focus is none other than Christ Jesus himself. We are to keep our eye on him at all times and be his apprentices. His command is simple: love God with all our hearts, souls, and minds, and love our neighbour as ourselves. The task is so simple and yet so difficult to actually do.

Isn't it true that we can get easily distracted from that real focus of life? We find ourselves consumed with the clothes we wear, with having the latest techno gadgets, with the car we drive, the house we live in, or the job we are employed to do. Yes, we can get so easily distracted from life's ultimate goal – to do the will of God in our lives and follow the example of Christ.

We are called to remain completely focused on the task at hand – live like Christ. It means that we are called to talk to that neighbour whom we don't like and haven't talked to in 20 years. It means that we are called to reach out in forgiveness to that sibling, parent, or child who hurt us many years ago. It means that we are called to act with kindness to those with whom we disagree personally or politically. It means we are called to love others to the extreme.

You see, when we come here each Sunday, some of us come out of obligation, others come to be nourished, and still others don't know why they are here at all. No matter the reason, we may be absolutely sure that as we leave, our focus is to live as Christ lived. We do not live the gospel here in this church; we live it in the real world of our day-to-day lives. We live it in the ordinary events of our complicated lives. We come to this table to be nourished, because we know that to live as Christ lived is hard work; we must not be distracted in any way, but remain focused on the task at hand. You see, in the end we will not be judged on how well we lived but how well we loved. We come to this table to hear the proclaimed Word, and to receive the real Christ, so that we can become Christ to others. May we be very sure of our focus, to speak as Christ spoke, to forgive as Christ forgave, to live as Christ lived, to love as Christ loved. Today, we come to be an apprentice of Christ.

Overcoming Fear to Become a Disciple

The great composer, Ludwig van Beethoven was not a man known for his social graces. He was said to be uncomfortable and often gruff with people.

There is a story told that when the son of his close friend died, Beethoven rushed over to his friend's home to express his profound grief. He had no words to offer, but for the next half hour, he sat at his friend's piano and expressed his emotions in the most eloquent way he could. When he had finished playing, the maestro simply got up and walked out.

His friend later said that no one else's visit meant as much to him and his family as the music that Beethoven played that day. It had expressed the inexpressible for Beethoven.[1]

Some of us possess great talents that are easily recognisable in music, literature, or other arts; in medicine, computers, or other sciences; others have more subtle talents in the ability to listen and offer encouragement and care, in support and healing, as we comfort others in pain. All of us have talents of one kind or another, gifted to us by our generous and loving God. We will not be judged on the greatness of our talents or gifts but on how well we used those talents or gifts. As Christian disciples, we are called to not only use our talents but to invest them and increase their worth. After they have increased, we are called to share them with others out of love and justice for all, for the greater good of our own community and the wider community of humanity. We are called to develop, use, and share our talents.

In today's gospel, Jesus tells us the parable of three servants, two of whom are considered good and faithful; the third is considered worthless and wicked. What is the difference between these servants? The difference is the way they used their talents. The first two servants took what had been given to them, and invested their talents and doubled their money. The third, out of fear of his master, buried his money because he believed that the master was a demanding man. Out of fear of his master, he did

---

1. 'Connections" (Mediaworks, Londonderry, NH: November 13, 2005)

nothing. The third servant was immobilised by fear. Sometimes, we do not use our gifts or talents out of fear. Sometimes, we bury our talents, too. I do not think we are in fear of the Lord as much as we fear the ridicule of others.

Let's take an example: say we had the gift of singing – a voice like an angel – but we never sang. It would be crazy not to use that gift. Imagine if Beethoven never wrote a note or played a tune. It would be absurd and the world would be deprived of beautiful and moving music. Yet, there are people here today who have gifts that they have never used. If we can sing we ought to sing. We might be afraid of what people would say. People might laugh at us for even thinking about it. We may not sound as great as we think. Maybe we are afraid of failing, but we have not tried yet! We may indeed have a great voice but we ought not expect to be the soloist immediately. Even Beethoven did not start out writing symphonies. He developed his skills later through his hard work. If we are able to sing, we probably need to train our voice, and develop that gift, so we can sing even better. We are never so far along that we cannot learn something new. Our gifts are constantly in need of development and training. When we have developed our talents, we are called to share them with others for the greater good of our wider community. Our talents may not be as great as a composer like Beethoven, or publicly recognisable as the gift of being able to sing, but we all have talents and gifts. We need to discover what they are and then develop them. So this week, may we really take the challenge to examine what gifts and talents God uniquely gives us. May we, then, take the task to really develop them. If we cannot recognise any talents, then maybe we go to someone to help identify those gifts. We will not only be judged as individuals, but also will be judged as a community, on how well we used our gifts. We need to help each other discover our gifts. We need to encourage every one to use those gifts for others. Then, we can become good and faithful servants of God.

This week, may we overcome our fear, and become good disciples by developing and using our talents for others. Because in the end, we will not be judged on the greatness of our talents or gifts but on how well we developed and used the gifts we have.

Removing the Earplugs of Life

After a few days on the job, the new security guard came home
despondent. Looking at his dejection his wife asked gently,
'What's wrong, honey?' 'I was fired,' he moaned. 'Oh my! What
happened?' his wife inquired. 'Well, when I was on duty at the
desk I dozed off for a moment, and while I was asleep someone
broke into the building and stole lots of computer equipment.'
'But honey, you're such a light sleeper. I'm surprised you didn't
wake up. There must have been some noise when the burglar
broke in.' 'I was not fired for falling asleep,' he confessed. 'I was
fired for wearing earplugs.'[1]

I believe we often do the same thing with our lives. We keep
our ears plugged so we can go through life without hearing the
sounds that disturb us. It may not be burglars but there are
sounds that could wake us from the sleepiness of our lives.

Today, we celebrate the Solemnity of Christ the King and one
of the main themes we hear in the gospel is that Christ will be
judge over all who come to him. We hear in this gospel not only
that he will judge us for what we do to our fellow human beings
but also what we fail to do for even the least of them. And we
hear a long list of things we are to do and people we are to care
for. To feed the hungry, give drink to the thirsty, clothe the
naked, shelter the homeless, and visit the sick and imprisoned.

Fundamentally, we are called to listen to the cries of the poor
or oppressed, to those who live on the margins of our society.
But we often put in our own earplugs and refuse to hear the cry
of the needy voice. We do this in small ways when we block out
the voice of our spouse or children when they really need to
share the story of the day. We also do this in bigger ways when
we block out the voices of the oppressed and underprivileged in
our society. It may be something as simple as when our spouse
or children talk and we tune them out. Or when the needy in our
society speak and we block them out because we are angry or
disagree with them. Or we simply don't make the effort to hear
them. We put in our earplugs! We live in a neighbourhood
where we do not have many poor people and so we do not hear

1. 'Connections' (Mediaworks, Londonderry, NH: November 13, 2005).

the cry of the poor. We hear on television, or see an article in the paper, about the immigrant workers' rights. We are angry there are so many illegal immigrants, so we choose to not hear the cries of injustice. We pretend that we do not hear these voices. The earplugs we use are often the busyness of our lives; we don't have a chance to hear. Yet, Christ will judge all according to our deeds: those done and those left undone!

But there is a more dominant theme in today's readings: the image of God as a good shepherd. The prophet Ezekiel reminds the people of Israel that even though their leaders have abandoned them, their God will lead them as a shepherd leads his flock. Then in the responsorial psalm we hear that the Lord is our Shepherd and there is nothing we shall want. And in the gospel, Jesus tells us how he separates us, like a shepherd separates the sheep from the goats. We are not an agricultural society and we might forget how this process actually happens. You see the shepherd would lead his flock by walking ahead and calling his sheep, often by name. His sheep, knowing his voice, would follow immediately. Any mountain goats that had gathered with the sheep would not follow because they would not recognise the voice. So you see, in the end, the judgement we receive is actually our own judgement on ourselves. For we will follow the voice of the One with whom we are familiar.

Our task, as Christians, is to listen and really hear that voice of the Saviour who calls us to follow him. We must attune ourselves to his voice so we can recognise it when he calls. We know that this is hard work for there are lots of competing voices. It is easy to come here and listen to God in our liturgy but we must live the liturgy in our daily lives. That is where the real work is – listening to God's voice in the midst of daily life. I believe that the voice of God often comes through the cries of the poor, oppressed, or underprivileged and it is hard to attune ourselves to those voices. But that is our Christian duty.

So this week as we reflect on our lives, maybe we need to remove the earplugs of frustration, anger, ambivalence or indifference so we can hear the voice of God speaking through the least in our society. This week, may we take our earplugs out and hear the voice of God through the cries of the poor.